GO!

*30 Meditations on How Best to Love
Your Neighbor as Yourself*

GO!

30 Meditations on How Best to Love
Your Neighbor as Yourself

Fr. John Bartunek, L.C., S.Th.D.

ministry23

Published by ministry23, LLC
2401 Harnish Drive, Ste 100
Algonquin, Illinois 60102
ministry23.com

Unless otherwise noted, Scripture passages are taken from the *New American Bible with Revised New Testament and Revised Psalms* © 1991, 1986, 1970 Confraternity of Christian Doctrine, Washington, D.C. and are used by permission of the copyright owner. All rights reserved.

Quotes marked *CCC* are taken from the English translation of the *Catechism of the Catholic Church for the United States of America*, 2nd ed. Copyright 1997 by United States Catholic Conference— Libreria Editrice Vaticana.

Cover design: Juliana Michelotti

ISBN 978-0-9965812-3-3

Printed in the United States of America

5 4 3 2 1

TABLE OF CONTENTS

Introduction

IF YOU ARE a follower of Christ, you have received a mission in this world. You are called not only to know and love God more and more, but also to be God's partner in bringing others to do the same, thereby lovingly helping them discover the "pearl of great price" (Matthew 13:46). Those two loves—love for God and love for neighbor—constitute the only path of true, lasting fulfillment. That's why Jesus summarized the meaning of human life by giving us the two greatest commandments:

> *One of the scribes, when he came forward and heard them disputing and saw how well he had answered them, asked [Jesus], "Which is the first of all the commandments?" Jesus replied, "The first is this: 'Hear, O Israel! The Lord our God is Lord alone! You shall love the Lord your God with all your heart, with all your soul, with all your mind, and with all your strength.' The second is this: 'You shall love your neighbor as yourself.' There is no other commandment greater than these."* (Mark 12:28–31)

In my previous book, *Seeking First the Kingdom: 30 Meditations on How to Love God with All Your Heart, Soul, Mind, and Strength,* we explored in detail the first great commandment and its implications for our day-to-day relationship with God. In this book we will explore the second: "You shall love your neighbor as yourself" (Mark 28:31).

The Connection Between Love and Mission

The essence of our mission in the world is to love as God loves—we are created in his image and likeness, and his nature is love (see 1 John 4:8), so our fulfillment flows from entering fully and consciously into the stream of divine love. Loving means, essentially, affirming the goodness of someone else's existence and doing good to that person in such a way that his or her existence can truly flourish. Love involves desiring, giving, and working to help others be all they can be, all God calls them to be. And since every human being is "made to live in communion with God, in whom he finds happiness" (*CCC*, 45), the best way to love someone is to help that person discover, establish, and deepen that communion with God.

That is our most basic and indispensible mission in the world; that is how we best fulfill the second great commandment and find the meaning we most yearn for. Pope Benedict XVI put it well:

> *To make Christ known is the most precious gift that you can give to others…. When you work to help others and proclaim the gospel to them, then your own lives, so often fragmented because of your many activities, will find their unity in the Lord. You will also build up your own selves, and you will grow and mature in humanity.* [1]

What You Can Expect to Get Out of This Book

Each person's mission of love unfolds in a unique and unrepeatable way, since each of us is a unique and unrepeatable person. Yet within that unique unfolding, certain elements and patterns are shared by all Christians. Jesus has told us a lot about them in the Gospels, and the Church has become more acutely aware of them through her two thousand years of being involved in this mission. These are the elements that this book will present and explain.

---

1 Pope Benedict XVI, Message for the Twenty-Eighth World Youth Day 2013.

Discovering them—or rediscovering and reflecting more deeply on them—is essential to being fully engaged in the Christian quest, and only full engagement in that quest will quench the existential thirst we have for meaning and happiness. We are created for more than simply making a living and trying to have a good time. And we all recognize that, deep down inside. Each of us is looking for the deeper meaning of our lives, and that meaning is connected with Christ's call to mission, with his call to making a lasting impact on the world by loving our neighbor as ourselves. The mission is there to be discovered, and this book can help.

Maybe, however, you already have been consciously engaged in spreading the message of Christ. Maybe you are an old hand at evangelization and apostolate (other names for the Church's mission), at sharing the faith, at finding creative and innovative ways to further the Church's goals, at sincerely and consistently seeking to love your neighbor as yourself on a daily basis. If so, this book is still for you.

A common—and spiritually dangerous—development in the life of conscious and intentional Christians is burnout. We can overextend ourselves, take on too many duties and responsibilities at the parish, for example, get involved in so many projects that they actually begin to interfere with our relationship with God, with our family life.… You might be thinking, *Aren't we called to save the world? Isn't that what the Church is all about? So don't I need to fill every waking moment with some kind of apostolic outreach?*

Yes and no. Yes, we are indeed called to do everything through, with, and in Christ, as St. Paul reminds us: "And whatever you do, in word or in deed, do everything in the name of the Lord Jesus, giving thanks to God the Father through him" (Colossians 3:17).

But no, frenetic and overcommitted activity is not the path to Christian maturity and fruitfulness. How can we properly discern how much we should take on, and how can we put a discordant, out-of-control life back in order and harmony? Reviewing the Church's vision for what we are each called to do and going back to our Lord's own teaching about the apostolate will help show the way.

How This Book Is Arranged

Not all Catholics realize they are called to be missionaries. Many of us simply assume that this aspect of the Church only has to do with priests, nuns, and other consecrated persons who have been called to explicit missionary status. The rest of us laypeople, so the misunderstanding goes, are off the hook. The first part of the book, "You Are Called," then, will address what the *Catechism* calls every Christian's "share in the priestly, prophetical, and kingly office of Christ… By Baptism they share in the priesthood of Christ, in his prophetic and royal mission" (*CCC*, 873, 1268).

Every Catholic truly is a missionary, and the first step to discovering and fulfilling our mission is to let that fact seep into our consciousness. The meditations in this first part focus on the call that each of us has received to be missionaries, evangelizers, apostles (as we will see, those terms are almost synonymous, though each has its own specific connotations)—to be part of the solution God wants to bring to the troubled world through his Church. You will have to be a little bit patient in Part One, since it requires dealing with some theological concepts that might appear to be abstract. But if we don't get those on the table right away, our missionary identity can never really take the firm root it needs to take in our self-awareness.

The universal call to mission, however, does not mean that every individual Christian should be searching through uncharted lands seeking to convert those who have never before heard of Jesus. That is only one kind of mission, though critical. Nor does it mean that every Christian has to have a PhD in theology. And so the second and third parts of this book ("Things to Keep in Mind" and "Your Modes of Apostolate") both explore some key presuppositions that will help us accept and rejoice in our call to be missionaries and also reflect on three dimensions of our Christian mission—the "priestly, prophetical, and kingly" dimensions that the *Catechism* refers to. Many readers will find surprises in this section as they discover how, as Christians, every single thing we do can have a missionary impact that reverberates into eternity. It's easier than you think to be the missionary you are called to be.

Having delved into our call to the apostolate in part 1, having cleared the air of some mistaken attitudes in part 2, and having explicated the different forms or dimensions in which we can and should fulfill our share in the apostolate in part 3, we will be ready to set a few expectations in part 4, "What to Expect." This part highlights some pitfalls and challenges that every Christian apostle has to face sooner or later. Jesus gives plenty of advice about dealing with these, and part 4 will serve up some healthy portions of it.

How to Use This Book Wisely

The ideas contained in this book are not new or complicated. They are basic ideas that make up our Christian identity. But they are ideas that all too often don't sink into our hearts—they stay in our heads. We agree with them, but we don't really allow them to have a deep impact on the way we see ourselves and the way we live our lives. That's why I decided to present them in the form of meditations. A meditation gives us a chance to take one or two critical ideas, reflect on them with calm focus, and allow them to penetrate our souls.

The division of this book's explanations and reflections into thirty short chapters is also meant to make it easy to use, either individually or in a small group. Reading prayerfully through one chapter a day can give you a monthlong spiritual retreat. The abundant biblical quotations are presented in red in order to make prayer and meditation on God's sacred Word easier, if you use the book in this way. Working through one chapter a week together with a group of friends can provide a richly rewarding path of Christ-centered fellowship for the better part of a year.

The questions for reflection at the end of each chapter can serve either as aids for personal reflection and prayer or as helps to spark invigorating small-group interaction. Each chapter's concluding prayer, drawn from various sources that make up the vast, two-thousand-year-old treasury of Christian spirituality, can be prayed individually or as a group. The introductory quotations from either canonized or beatified popes are meant to focus the reader's attention on the chapter's theme, as well as to reinforce the message by showing how deeply rooted these ideas are in the Church's self-understanding.

Jesus's last words before his ascension into heaven launched the Church on her mission. "Go!" he commanded:

> *"Go, therefore, and make disciples of all nations, baptizing them in the name of the Father, and of the Son, and of the Holy Spirit, teaching them to observe all that I have commanded you." (Matthew 28:19–20)*

This passage is known by tradition as the "Great Commission," and in a sense it sets the Christian quest in motion; it shows us how best to obey Jesus's earlier commandment to "love your neighbor as yourself." Let's start there.

PART I
You Are Called

"The kingdom of heaven is like a landowner who went out at dawn to hire laborers for his vineyard. After agreeing with them for the usual daily wage, he sent them into his vineyard. Going out about nine o'clock, he saw others standing idle in the marketplace, and he said to them, 'You too go into my vineyard, and I will give you what is just.' So they went off.… [And] he went out again around noon, and around three o'clock, and did likewise. Going out about five o'clock, he found others standing around, and said to them, 'Why do you stand here idle all day?' They answered, 'Because no one has hired us.' He said to them, 'You too go into my vineyard.' When it was evening the owner of the vineyard said to his foreman, 'Summon the laborers and give them their pay, beginning with the last and ending with the first…'" (Matthew 20:1–3, 5–8)

Chapter 1
There Is Work to Do

The gospel parable sets before our eyes the Lord's vast vineyard and the multitude of persons, both women and men, who are called and sent forth by him to labor in it. The vineyard is the whole world (cf. Mt 13:38), which is to be transformed according to the plan of God in view of the final coming of the Kingdom of God.
—St. John Paul II, *Christifideles Laici,* 1

IN THE EARLY Church, some fresh Christian converts had the wrong idea of how Christ's followers were supposed to behave in this world. They focused so much on Jesus's promise to come again and bring human history to its fulfillment that they unplugged themselves from normal life. They idly awaited the Lord's Second Coming, refraining from any productive activity besides prayer. This caused problems, as can be imagined, for the Christian communities. St. Paul actually had to address it explicitly in one of his letters, correcting those Christians in Thessalonica who were remiss in even the most basic responsibility to make a living:

> *In fact, when we were with you, we instructed you that if anyone was unwilling to work, neither should that one eat. We hear that some are conducting themselves among you in a disorderly way, by not keeping busy but minding*

the business of others. Such people we instruct and urge in the Lord Jesus Christ to work quietly and to eat their own food. But you, brothers, do not be remiss in doing good. (2 Thessalonians 3:10–13)

Hearts in Heaven—Feet on the Ground

This problem has cropped up at various times in the history of the Church. Outsiders criticized members of the Church for being so focused on the life to come that they disengaged from life here on earth. Perhaps in certain cases the criticism was valid. Yet the actual doctrine of the Church has always stressed the importance of Christians staying engaged in earthly life in order to redeem human experience and shape it in accordance with God's wise plan. Here is how the Second Vatican Council expressed the critics' point of view in its modern context:

Not to be overlooked among the forms of modern atheism is that which anticipates the liberation of man especially through his economic and social emancipation. This form argues that by its nature religion thwarts this liberation by arousing man's hope for a deceptive future life, thereby diverting him from the constructing of the earthly city. [1]

And here is how that same Council asserted the proper understanding of the relationship between hope in heaven and active engagement here on earth:

This council exhorts Christians, as citizens of two cities, to strive to discharge their earthly duties conscientiously and in response to the gospel spirit. They are mistaken who, knowing that we have here no abiding city but seek one which is to come, think that they may therefore shirk their earthly responsibilities. For they are forgetting

---

1 Second Vatican Council, *Gaudium et Spes*, 21.

that by the faith itself they are more obliged than ever to measure up to these duties, each according to his proper vocation. [2]

In other words, Christians should be hard workers. A follower of Christ knows that this earthly life is an opportunity to develop one's potential and make a difference in the world. As Christian disciples, that opportunity is the arena we are given to exercise our love, to show and grow our commitment to God and neighbor by putting our lives and talents at the service of others.

A Fruitful Partnership

The landowner in the parable of the vineyard goes out to look for workers, and he gives them work: "You too go into my vineyard." The vineyard image appears throughout the history of salvation as recorded in the Bible. As St. John Paul II pointed out: "The vineyard is the whole world (cf. Matthew 13:38), which is to be transformed according to the plan of God in view of the final coming of the Kingdom of God."

The vineyard is a powerful image for the Christian adventure, even on a merely natural level. The Lord owns the vineyard, and the Lord gives the vines the power to produce grapes. He also provides the sunshine, air, and water the vine need to grow and bear fruit. But those God-given elements will only reach their full potential through cultivation by human beings. The vineyard needs intense labor from many workers in order to produce the fine wine it is capable of producing.

It is no coincidence that Jesus's first miracle consisted of turning water into wine. In a sense, the reproduction of that miracle throughout history is the primary work of the Church. Through the cultivation of the vineyard of the world, the Church infuses God's grace into human affairs, transforming the basic elements of the

---

2 Ibid., 43.

earthly community into the fine wine of *"a chosen race, a royal priesthood, a holy nation, a people of his own"* (1 Peter 2:9).

Our Best Work

There truly is work to do—both normal earthly work that needs to be seasoned with Christian love and grace in order to reach its full potential, as well as the more directly supernatural work of spreading faith in Jesus Christ. This is the work Jesus calls us all to engage in by sending us into his vineyard. This is the work his Church was established to accomplish.

And it is this work that will give the deepest meaning to our lives. As Pope Francis explained it:

> *When the Church summons Christians to take up the task of evangelization, she is simply pointing to the source of authentic personal fulfillment. For here we discover a profound law of reality: that life is attained and matures in the measure that it is offered up in order to give life to others. This is certainly what mission means.*[3]

And so the Church wisely and lovingly invites each one of us, today and every day, to take our unique place in the vineyard of the Lord:

> *The mission of salvation is universal; for every person and for the whole person. It is a task which involves the entire People of God, all the faithful. Mission must therefore be the passion of every Christian; a passion for the salvation of the world and ardent commitment to work for the coming of the Father's kingdom.*[4]

---

3 Pope Francis, *Evangelii Gaudium*, 10.
4 St. John Paul II, Message for World Mission Sunday, 9; October 24, 1999.

Questions for Personal Reflection or Group Discussion

1. What idea in this chapter struck you most and why?

2. How fully do you feel part of this work that God has given us to do? In other words, to what extent do you feel you are working in the Lord's vineyard?

3. When you think about this work the Church is called to be engaged in, how does it make you feel? Excited, eager, intimidated, overwhelmed? Why do you think you feel that way?

4. Various secular sociological studies point out that an important ingredient for a happy life is meaningful work. This coheres with the biblical account of the creation of man and woman. When God created us, he gave us work to do—"to cultivate and care for" the earth (Genesis 2:15). Our very nature requires that we feel in some way useful and productive in order to feel fulfilled. The rest of this book will explore the different ways God gives us for meeting this fundamental need as completely as possible. But for today, how will you raise your awareness of this need and seek to fulfill it more healthily?

•   I will take time to think about how even my most mundane activities can be useful and meaningful in in God's eyes, and I will try to live them with a greater sense of purpose.

•   I will identify one of my talents or gifts that tends to be underutilized and find a way to make it productive today.

•   I will reflect on which of my duties and responsibilities seem to be the least fulfilling to me and try to figure out why. Then I will commit to a practical or attitudinal adjustment that may help them become more fulfilling and meaningful.

•   (Write your own commitment) I will _____

Concluding Prayer

O God, Creator of all things,
who laid down for the human race the law of work,
graciously grant that
by the example of Saint Joseph and under his patronage
we may complete the works you set us to do
and attain the rewards you promise.

—*Roman Missal,* Collect for May 1, Feast of St. Joseph the Worker

Chapter 2
The Church's Deepest Identity

Evangelizing is in fact the grace and vocation proper to the Church, her deepest identity. She exists in order to evangelize, that is to say, in order to preach and teach, to be the channel of the gift of grace, to reconcile sinners with God, and to perpetuate Christ's sacrifice in the Mass, which is the memorial of His death and glorious resurrection.

—Blessed Pope Paul VI, *Evangelii Nuntiandi*, 14

WHEN YOU THINK of the Catholic Church, what's the first thing that comes to mind? For many, the Catholic Church is primarily an organization. It has a hierarchical structure that moves from a local parish priest up to a local bishop and then all the way up to the pope, the head of the Church. And all the individuals who call themselves "Catholics" are members of that organization, similar to the way soldiers are members of an army, or college students are members of a fraternity or a sorority.

That is true, as far as it goes. The Catholic Church is an organization, with a structured hierarchy and a wide membership. Yet to think of the Church primarily in that way is like thinking of a human being only as a skeleton holding together different muscle groups and biological systems, not as a real *person*. The concept is too reductive.

More Than Just an Organization

What does this organization do? Where does it come from? Where is it going? What is its purpose? And what characterizes the Church's members? These questions point toward a more robust understanding of the Church's identity—and therefore a more robust understanding of our own identity as Catholics.

And at the core of everything is the Church's mission to spread the gospel: "Evangelizing is in fact the grace and vocation proper to the Church, her deepest identity. She exists in order to evangelize…"

The word *evangelization* can be used in many different ways, but we need to distill it down to an essential meaning in order to achieve clarity in our search for understanding the commandment to love our neighbors as ourselves. Here is how the *Catechism's* glossary defines evangelization: "the proclamation of Christ and his gospel (Greek: *evangelion*) by word and the testimony of life, in fulfillment of Christ's command."[1]

The Greek word *evangelion* literally means "good news." From it derive the English words *evangelist*, which means one who proclaims the good news, and *evangelize*, which means to proclaim or spread the good news, and other cognates like *evangelism* and *evangelization*. The English word *gospel* is a translation of those terms. Just as *gospel* in Old English comes from two words meaning "good story," so the original Greek word comes from two words meaning "good announcement, or news." Latin adopted the Greek word itself, Latinizing it into *evangelium* and sometimes translated it literally into *bona anuntiatio*. The same Greek root gives us our word *angels*, the spiritual beings who often serve as God's "announcers" or messengers throughout the history of salvation.

In the early years of Christianity, the word *evangelion* referred

---

1 Libreria Editrice Vaticana (2011-11-02). *Catechism of the Catholic Church* (Kindle Locations 27410–27411). United States Conference of Catholic Bishops. Kindle edition.

primarily to all the Church's activity of spreading and promoting the Christian faith and message (the content of the "good news"). And since all Christians were involved in that activity, all Christians were evangelizers. Eventually the four authors of the written accounts of Jesus's life and ministry were referred to as Evangelists in a more technical sense, and their individual accounts were entitled Gospels (the Gospel according to Matthew, Mark, Luke, or John).

Today these technical senses are the most well known, and unfortunately that reflects a general diminishment of the everyday Catholic's understanding of the Church's true mission. After all, if the four Evangelists have already written down the gospel definitively in the Gospels, then what's all this talk about evangelization? It's already happened, hasn't it?

The Dynamism of Evangelization

Yes and no. This particular piece of good news is more than simple information, though it includes information. The Word of God— what God speaks to us and announces to us in Jesus—is actually alive. It takes root and grows, like a seed, bearing spiritual fruit and transforming human lives, communities, and cultures. The Book of Hebrews alludes to this:

> *Indeed, the word of God is living and effective, sharper than any two-edged sword, penetrating even between soul and spirit, joints and marrow, and able to discern reflections and thoughts of the heart.* (Hebrews 4:12)

So the gospel, the good news about the salvation of sinners through God's grace and mercy, refers to something that has indeed already happened (the coming of Jesus Christ and the accomplishment of his mission on earth). But it also refers to something that is ongoing: a multi-dimensional process of spreading this grace and mercy that will continue until the very end of history, when Jesus comes again to put an end to all evil and suffering.

The Dimensions of Evangelization

The work of evangelization, then, the spreading of the gospel, involves three basic activities, and engaging in these activities constitutes the deepest identity of the Church. The Church's organization is at the service of these activities, of this mission that announces and promotes the good news of Jesus Christ. Here are the three dimensions or "moments" of evangelization:

- *Spreading the knowledge of Jesus Christ and his saving mission to those who have not yet heard about it.* This is traditionally called the "mission *ad gentes,*" which is Latin for "to the peoples." Many times, when we think of missionaries, we think of people who are primarily engaged in this work of spreading the gospel to those corners of the world that haven't yet heard it even for the first time. Though a critical dimension of evangelization, this is not the only sector of missionary activity.

- *Instructing and initiating into the life of the Church those who have heard and accepted the gospel but are not yet mature in their faith.* The traditional term most often associated with this work is *catechesis* (another word with Greek roots—this time the Greek origin refers to "instruction by word of mouth").

- *Cultivation toward full spiritual maturity and fruitfulness of the seed of grace in the lives of those who have received it,* such that it transforms individuals, families, communities, and entire cultures in harmony with God's will for the human family. This is often referred to as the work of *sanctification,* or "making holy."[2]

The Church's mission is to evangelize, and evangelization involves all these dimensions, along with all their logical corollaries and implications: "The Church 'exists in order to evangelize'; that is

---

2 For this tripartite description of the Church's evangelizing mission, see the Vatican Congregation for the Clergy, *General Directory for Catechesis,* 49.

the carrying forth of the Good News to every sector of the human race so that by its strength it may enter into the hearts of men and renew the human race."[3]

This is what the twelve apostles and the rest of Christ's first followers were sent out to do by the Lord; it is the Church's reason for being.

> He [Jesus] said to them, "Go into the whole world and proclaim the gospel to every creature." (Mark 16:15)

In fact, the word *mission* comes from the Latin word for "sent out" (*missio*), which in Greek is related to *apostello,* the same root that gives us *apostle* and *apostolate*. Mission, evangelization, spreading the gospel, apostolate—this lexicon begins to unveil the richness of the Church's deepest identity—which, as we will see in the next meditation, also gives us a clue about our own deepest identity.

Questions for Personal Reflection or Group Discussion

1. What idea in this chapter struck you most and why?

2. When you think about the Catholic Church, what images or concepts come spontaneously to mind? Why? What do they tell you about your attitude toward the Church?

3. Try to explain in your own words the different nuances of these terms related to the Church's deepest identity: mission, evangelization, apostolate, gospel.

4. The concept of evangelization is so rich that it can't really be defined exhaustively with mathematical precision. The Vatican's *General Directory for Catechesis* points out: "However, no such definition can be accepted for that complex, rich and dynamic reality which is called evangelization. There is the risk

---

3 Vatican Congregation for the Clergy, *General Directory for Catechesis*, 46; vatican.va.

of impoverishing it or even of distorting it…. Evangelization must be viewed as the process by which the Church, moved by the Spirit, proclaims and spreads the gospel throughout the entire world" (46–48). Considering how rich and multidimensional this reality is, what will you do today to engage more intentionally in the Church's work of evangelization?

- I will make a visit to the Eucharist and pray for missionaries who are struggling against taxing and dangerous difficulties.

- I will take five minutes to write a thank you note to God for all the evangelizers whose efforts went into my receiving the Catholic faith (try to list as many of those people as you can think of).

- I will get together with a friend and talk about how the Church in my area is continuing the work of evangelization. Then I will pray for the success of those efforts and brainstorm about how I can join in.

- (Write your own commitment) I will_____

Concluding Prayer

O God, in the covenant of your Christ
you never cease to gather to yourself from all nations
a people growing together in unity through the Spirit;
grant, we pray, that your Church,
faithful to the mission entrusted to her,
may continually go forward with the human family
and always be the leaven and the soul of human society,
to renew it in Christ and transform it into the family of God.

—*Roman Missal,* Collect for Mass for the Church, B

Chapter 3
You Too Go into My Vineyard!

"You go too." The call is a concern not only of pastors, clergy, and men and women religious. The call is addressed to everyone: lay people as well are personally called by the Lord, from whom they receive a mission on behalf of the Church and the world.... The voice of the Lord clearly resounds in the depths of each of Christ's followers, who through faith and the sacraments of Christian initiation is made like to Jesus Christ, is incorporated as a living member in the Church and has an active part in her mission of salvation.

—St. John Paul II, *Christifideles Laici*, 2–3

DEEP WITHIN EVERY human heart burns a desire for lasting purpose, for a truly meaningful life. In some hearts, this desire burns quietly, like a small ember waiting under thick layers of cold ash. People in that condition may try to fill their lives with earthly comforts and achievements, thinking that those things will be enough to satisfy them. They try to ignore or quench the deeper yearning.

In other hearts the desire flames out violently, impatiently belittling anything that doesn't directly contribute to whatever particular cause such individuals have dedicated themselves to. In this case, life can lose its balance and harmony, and people can turn even legitimate and necessary human works (i.e., curing cancer, ending world hunger) into a kind of idol. This can even lead to violence and destruction when the adopted cause or chosen means to promote it contradicts human dignity. Killing people in order to save an endangered animal or plant species, for example, is dangerously off-kilter.

The Source of Meaning

Neither earthly comforts and achievements nor ideological idols can fulfill the longings of the human heart. Our hearts are made for God and his kingdom, for everlasting life. Nothing on this side of eternity can truly satisfy them. Here we can only begin to experience the fullness of life to which God is leading us, but even that beginning is far superior to anything the secular world can give us.

God wants us to find and follow that path of true meaning. He wants us to experience the growing fullness of life that comes with following that path. In fact, Jesus summed up his life's mission in those terms: "I came that they might have life, and have it more abundantly" (John 10:10).

Being evangelized by the Church gives us access to this path. It actually sets us on "the road that leads to life" (Matthew 7:14) by uniting us to the source of life himself—Jesus.

Through baptism we become members of this Church that is Christ still present in the world, renewing and redeeming the human family from within. Our spiritual DNA is enhanced by baptism, so that in a sense every Christian becomes another Christ. As St. Cyprian put it way back in the third century: "*Christianus alter Christus*"—"Every Christian is another Christ." The other sacraments nourish that divine life of Christ in each baptized person, as does the instruction and guidance that each receives from more mature members of the Church—parents, teachers, priests, and so on.

Healthy Plants Bear Fruit

The healthy growth of this divine life of grace tends irresistibly to produce fruit. Healthy Christians naturally share with others the gifts of grace they have received. As they grow to spiritual maturity, they produce spiritual fruit analogous to how mature plants produce material fruit. Jesus used this image to describe the growth of his kingdom:

> *He said, "This is how it is with the kingdom of God; it is as if a man were to scatter seed on the land and would sleep and rise night and day and the seed would sprout and grow, he knows not how. Of its own accord the land yields fruit, first the blade, then the ear, then the full grain in the ear. And when the grain is ripe, he wields the sickle at once, for the harvest has come." (Mark 4:26–29)*

A healthy seed grows and bears fruit—that's what it does. The seed of grace, according to the Lord, is no different. The urge to help others live life to the fullest, the desire to help them discover the liberating truths of the gospel and experience the revitalizing mercy and love of Jesus Christ, surges up from within every mature Christian. It's part of who we are. It's a spiritual vital sign.

The classic expressions of this yearning to spread the love we have been given are found strewn throughout the New Testament writings of St. Paul, the quintessential missionary. "For the love of Christ impels us," he wrote to the Christians in Corinth (2 Corinthians 5:14). In a previous letter, he had explained his own sense of mission with another phrase that has been taken up by every Christian generation since: "If I preach the gospel, this is no reason for me to boast, for an obligation has been imposed on me, and woe to me if I do not preach it!" (1 Corinthians 9:16).

People versus Plants

Of course, human beings are different than plants. Plants grow and bear fruit unconsciously. In the spiritual life, however, growth and fruitfulness are linked to our free cooperation, to our decision to listen and obey as "the voice of Lord clearly resounds in the depths" of our souls, to quote St. John Paul II again. As baptized Christians we are evangelizers in our very nature, but we are capable of denying that nature, of starving it or hiding it or otherwise acting against it. When we do so, we impede the Church's mission, we fail in our call to love, and we deviate from the path of meaning that alone will satisfy the deepest longings of our heart.

Jesus's description of this missionary aspect of our Christian identity illustrates both these dimensions—that we are evangelizers by nature ever since our baptism, but that we can act against that nature. During his Sermon on the Mount, for example, he explained:

> *"You are the salt of the earth. But if salt loses its taste, with what can it be seasoned? It is no longer good for anything but to be thrown out and trampled underfoot. You are the light of the world. A city set on a mountain cannot be hidden. Nor do they light a lamp and then put it under a bushel basket; it is set on a lampstand, where it gives light to all in the house. Just so, your light must shine before others, that they may see your good deeds and glorify your heavenly Father." (Matthew 5:13–16)*

Christ's followers *are* the salt of the earth and the light of the world. Our identity involves bringing flavor and illumination to a world deadened and darkened by sin. As St. John Paul II said:

> *God calls me and sends me forth as a laborer in his vineyard. He calls me and sends me forth to work for the coming of his Kingdom in history. This personal vocation and mission defines the dignity and the responsibility of each member of the lay faithful.[4]*

And yet it is possible for us to become insipid salt or obscured light.

---

4 St. John Paul II, *Christifideles Laici*, 58.

As members of the Church, we are sharers in her mission, but we have to decide to live in accordance with that identity, to let our light shine before others and thus fulfill the commandment of love. That's what we are created to do, that's what we are called to do, that's what the world needs us to do, and that's what will satisfy our existential thirst for lasting fulfillment—for making a truly meaningful contribution to history. When the Lord of the vineyard looks at you and says, "You too go into my vineyard" (Matthew 20:4), he says it with a warm, eager, loving smile.

Questions for Personal Reflection or Group Discussion

1. What idea in this chapter struck you most and why?

2. When have you experienced most acutely the thirst for meaning and purpose God has placed in the depths of your soul? What did you do about it?

3. How deeply do you identify with this aspect of being a follower of Christ? How does your condition of being a missionary, being salt and light for the world, make you feel? Why?

4. Becoming aware of this missionary dimension can be overwhelming. We don't always feel up to such a high calling. We don't always feel properly equipped, trained, gifted, or talented. And yet the fact remains that we all share "the common vocation of all Christ's disciples, a vocation to holiness and to the mission of evangelizing the world" (CCC, 1533). In coming chapters we will explore the many different ways that mission can be lived out, which can help it be less overwhelming. But for today, how will you consciously express this core aspect of your deepest identity and deepest source of meaning?

- I will visit my parish church and take a few moments to reflect on all the artwork and decoration inside of it, asking myself what those images say to me about my identity as a Christian missionary.

- I will read a description of the life of my favorite saint, paying special attention to how that person lived out the missionary dimension of being a Christian.

- I will bring up my faith in a conversation where it wouldn't usually come up, even if indirectly, and see how God uses that.

- (Write your own resolution) I will_____

Concluding Prayer

O God, you have willed that your Church
be the sacrament of salvation for all nations,
so that Christ's saving work may continue to the end of the ages;
stir up, we pray, the hearts of your faithful
and grant that they may feel a more urgent call
to work for the salvation of every creature,
so that from all the peoples on earth
one family and one people of your own
may arise and increase.
Through our Lord Jesus Christ, your Son,
who lives and reigns with you in the unity of the Holy Spirit,
one God, for ever and ever.

—*Roman Missal,* Collect for the Mass for the Evangelization of Peoples

Chapter 4
Thy Kingdom Come!

The kingdom is the concern of everyone: individuals, society, and the world. Working for the kingdom means acknowledging and promoting God's activity, which is present in human history and transforms it. Building the kingdom means working for liberation from evil in all its forms. In a word, the kingdom of God is the manifestation and the realization of God's plan of salvation in all its fullness.

—St. John Paul II, *Redemptoris Missio,* 15

WHEN JESUS BEGAN preaching his message to the world, he referred to a kingdom:

> *Jesus came to Galilee proclaiming the gospel of God: "This is the time of fulfillment. The kingdom of God is at hand. Repent, and believe in the gospel." (Mark 1:14–15)*

When Jesus taught his disciples to pray, he instructed them to aim all their desires at that same kingdom:

> *"This is how you are to pray: Our Father in heaven, hallowed be your name, your kingdom come, your will be done, on earth as in heaven…" (Matthew 6:9–10)*

When Jesus's enemies turned him in to the Roman authorities, they charged him with trying to set up an independent kingdom in opposition to the Roman emperor. Pontius Pilate, the Roman governor at the time, asked Jesus if this accusation was true. The Lord answered, in the most critical moment of his life, by affirming that he was indeed a king, and that his kingdom was utterly unique.

Jesus answered, "My kingdom does not belong to this world. If my kingdom did belong to this world, my attendants [would] be fighting to keep me from being handed over to the Jews. But as it is, my kingdom is not here." (John 18:36)

Jesus linked the spreading of his message—the spreading of the gospel, the work of evangelization—to his kingdom. In this sense, the work of evangelization can be described as the work of building up Christ's kingdom—"working for the kingdom" and "building the kingdom" as St. John Paul II put it.

Kings and Fairy Tales

Some people consider this concept out of date. In the postmodern world, they say, kings and queens are obsolete. Even the ones who still survive are mere figureheads, symbols of archaic and irrelevant glory. To think of Christ as a king and the Church on earth as the "seed and beginning of [his] kingdom" (*CCC*, 541), these critics claim, is to mistakenly relegate Christianity to the realm of fairy tales.

And yet, as we have seen, Jesus used this concept continually. And the Church's official teaching has done the same, even into our own day. In fact, at the beginning of the postmodern era, when the human family was being thrown into historically unparalleled cataclysms of totalitarianism, world wars, global depression, genocides, and massive religious persecution, the Church invoked Christ's kingship as a rallying cry to restore a vestige of sanity.

In 1925 Pope Pius XI instituted throughout the whole Church the Feast of Christ the King. Its official liturgical name is now the Solemnity of Our Lord Jesus Christ, the King of the Universe. We are all familiar with it, since we celebrate it every year on the last Sunday before Advent—the Sunday that brings the liturgical year to its close. But we may be less familiar with the reasons behind its establishment.

Christ's Kingdom as the Soul of the World

Pius XI recognized that the ills of a decadent Western civilization, which were beginning to infect the rest of the world, were linked to a philosophical and cultural rejection of God and Jesus Christ. The modern world began to put its faith more in mankind—and mankind's ability to control its circumstances through science and technology—than in God and the wisdom of the gospel. As a result secularization advanced throughout countries whose popular culture for centuries had been imbued with a Christian worldview and Christian values. Here is how Pope Pius XI explained it in his second encyclical letter, which established the Feast of Christ the King:

> In the first Encyclical Letter which we addressed at the beginning of our pontificate to the bishops of the universal Church, we referred to the chief causes of the difficulties under which mankind was laboring. And we remember saying that these manifold evils in the world were due to the fact that the majority of men had thrust Jesus Christ and his holy law out of their lives; that these had no place either in private affairs or in politics: and we said further, that as long as individuals and states refused to submit to the rule of our Savior, there would be no really hopeful prospect of a lasting peace among nations.[5]

---

5 Pius XI, *Quas Primas*, 1.

By instituting the liturgical celebration of Christ the King, the Holy Father hoped to set up a counteroffensive to this insidious cultural trend of secularization. He hoped to remind all Catholics of their primary allegiance to a kingdom that is not limited to this passing world, a kingdom that allows the human spirit to flourish instead of flounder, because it leads people to live in obedience to the infinite wisdom and merciful love of Jesus. Only a life in harmony with God's will, in other words, can restore order and sanity to a world gone mad.

> *This kingdom is spiritual and concerned with spiritual things…. When once men recognize, both in private and in public life, that Christ is King, society will at last receive the great blessings of real liberty, well-ordered discipline, peace and harmony… That these blessings may be abundant and lasting in Christian society, it is necessary that the kingship of our Savior should be as widely as possible recognized and understood, and to that end nothing would serve better than the institution of a special feast in honor of the Kingship of Christ.[6]*

Letting Christ Reign in Every Sector of the Human Soul

This reminder and celebration, enshrined in the liturgy, could both help inoculate Catholics against the virus of secularization and also spur them on to live as faithful subjects and followers of the Lord.

> *The faithful, moreover, by meditating upon these truths, will gain much strength and courage, enabling them to form their lives after the true Christian ideal… [I]t must be clear that not one of our faculties is exempt from his empire. He must reign in our minds, which should assent with perfect submission and firm belief to revealed truths and to the doctrines of Christ. He must reign in our wills,*

---

6 Ibid., 15, 19, 21.

which should obey the laws and precepts of God. He must reign in our hearts, which should spurn natural desires and love God above all things, and cleave to him alone. He must reign in our bodies and in our members, which should serve as instruments for the interior sanctification of our souls, or to use the words of the Apostle Paul, as instruments of justice unto God. If all these truths are presented to the faithful for their consideration, they will prove a powerful incentive to perfection.[7]

Christ's kingdom comes whenever a person hears his message of truth and heeds his loving, redeeming will. This is why Jesus linked these two phrases in the Our Father: "Thy Kingdom come; thy will be done…"

Using the phrase "to build up the kingdom of Christ" as an expression of what the Church seeks to do through her evangelizing efforts has a profound benefit. It keeps us grounded in a fundamental truth, a truth easy to forget in a post-Christian world—namely, that we are not God, that the power of redemption and renewal that flows from the gospel comes not from us, who are merely messengers, but from the Lord. He is the king of the universe, and it is the grace of his kingdom that frees humble and obedient hearts from the deadening and destructive shackles of meaninglessness, falsehood, and sin. The mission of the Church, and the mission of each Christian, is to extend the breadth and the depth of that kingdom, the only kingdom that will last forever.

Questions for Personal Reflection or Group Discussion

1. What idea in this chapter struck you the most and why?

2. Express in your own words how the specific concept "building

---

7 Ibid., 33.

the kingdom of Christ" contributes to the general concept of evangelization.

3. When you use your imagination to picture Christ as the perfect king who is, through his Church, building up an eternal kingdom, how does it make you feel? Why? How does it make you feel to picture yourself as a member of this kingdom and a partner of the king in building it?

4. In early twentieth-century Mexico, a rabidly secularized government initiated a violent persecution of the Catholic Church. This led to the confiscation of Church property, the expulsion of clergy, and a general attempt to extinguish the practice of the Catholic faith. Catholics resisted this persecution, both peacefully and violently. The clash led to a decade of deadly unrest that witnessed, in addition to pitched battles between government forces and a Catholic citizen militia dubbed the "Cristeros," public executions and gruesome martyrdoms of clergy and laity throughout the nation. The Church has beatified many of these martyrs, including a young fourteen-year-old boy named José Sanchez del Río. Perhaps the most famous martyr from this era is the Jesuit priest, Blessed Miguel Pro. In many cases, the martyrs would be killed by a firing squad, and right before the final order to shoot was given, they would lift their voices with the Cristero battle cry: "¡Viva Cristo Rey!" ("Long live Christ the King!"). These martyrs refused to abandon their allegiance to Jesus and his kingdom, even at the cost of their lives. Today, how will you live out your faithfulness to Jesus, your Savior and King?

• I will make time to go to confession, using that sacrament both to confess my sins and to renew my desire to follow Jesus and live under the guidance of his wisdom and love.

• I will reach out to someone I know who is struggling with his or her faith, being for that person a reflection of God's goodness and interest.

- I will take some extra quiet time in prayer to ask the Lord how he wants me to contribute to building up his kingdom. I will say yes to whatever he asks of me.

- (Write your own resolution) I will _____

Concluding Prayer

O God, who in your wonderful providence
decreed that Christ's kingdom
should be extended throughout the earth
and that all should become partakers of his saving redemption,
grant, we pray, that your Church
may be the universal sacrament of salvation
and that Christ may be revealed to all
as the hope of the nations and their Savior.

—*Roman Missal,* Collect from the Mass for the Church, A

Chapter 5
The Motor of the Mission

Mother and Teacher of all nations—such is the Catholic Church in the mind of her Founder, Jesus Christ; to hold the world in an embrace of love, that men, in every age, should find in her their own completeness in a higher order of living, and their ultimate salvation. She is "the pillar and ground of the truth" (1 Timothy 3:15). To her was entrusted by her holy Founder the twofold task of giving life to her children and of teaching them and guiding them—both as individuals and as nations—with maternal care.

—St. John XXIII, *Mater et Magister,* 1

SOME PEOPLE WANT to conquer the world because they are megalomaniacs. Conquest is all about extending their egos, manifesting their power through domination of others. These are the would-be emperors of earthly kingdoms who will stop at nothing to achieve their goal—Napoleon, Stalin, Hitler. Every age of human history has figures like these. They echo the devil's own rebellious self-assertion, recorded in Scripture as a snapshot of the attitude behind sin in general: "Long ago you broke your yoke, you tore off your bonds. You said, 'I will not serve'" (Jeremiah 2:20).

Some critics of Christianity accuse Jesus, as the Church presents him, of being just one more of these. The leaders of the Catholic Church, according to them, seek to control and dominate people, to enslave them with the chains of ignorance and superstition through a millennia-long exercise in self-aggrandizement.

A Difference in Motivation

But that is not what Jesus's command to "Go, therefore, and make disciples of all nations!" is all about. That is not the goal of evangelization—not at all. Jesus—unlike the dictators whose failed totalitarian regimes litter the floor of human history—acted out of love. He is, in fact, the revelation of God's unlimited, unconditional love: "For God so loved the world that he gave his only Son, so that everyone who believes in him might not perish but might have eternal life" (John 3:16).

Evil dictators may not be fully responsible for their atrocities. Their psychological brokenness may absolve them from much of their culpability—or it may not; that is for God to judge. Yet in every case, they seek to enlarge themselves—their image, their reputation, their influence, their power—at the expense of others. They use others.

This contradicts true, Christlike love. The example and teaching of Jesus was the exact opposite. He gave himself, literally, for the sake of those he loved—all of us. He lowered himself to take on human nature through the Incarnation. He lived an obscure, working-class life in Nazareth for thirty years. He exhausted himself preaching, healing, and teaching his followers during his three years of public ministry. And he offered his own life in loving obedience unto death on a cross to atone for the sins of each and every member of the human family. He summed up his own earthly mission by saying: "…[T]he Son of Man did not come to be served but to serve and to give his life as a ransom for many" (Matthew 20:28).

A High Purpose for a Heartfelt Command

When Jesus commanded his apostles to make disciples of all nations, then, that command didn't flow from megalomania. It flowed from love, from the sincere, heartfelt desire to rescue every human soul from the existential frustration that is our natural inheritance due to original sin. His life and mission fulfilled the Old Testament prophecy:

> *The people who walked in darkness have seen a great light; upon those who lived in a land of gloom light has shone. You have brought them abundant joy and great rejoicing… (Isaiah 9:1–2)*

Jesus desires people to believe in him, follow him, and obey his teachings because he wants them to live life to the full: "I came that they might have life, and have it more abundantly" (John 10:10). He knows that all of the good things of the earth—wealth, pleasure, popularity, achievements, power—cannot satisfy the human heart. And when we seek to fill our hearts with them, they become twisted, destructive idols that actually thwart our progress toward fulfillment. Following them and putting our hopes in them, we become lost, confused, desperate, even twisted ourselves. Jesus alone, through the gift of divine grace, can save us from that, and he wants to do so; that's why he established a missionary Church.

Seeking the Troubled and Abandoned

This deep connection between love and mission comes across beautifully in a passage from St. Matthew's Gospel. Jesus had finished his Sermon on the Mount, and he had proven the trustworthiness of the words in that sermon by an astonishing series of miracles. At that point, St. Matthew gives us a glimpse into what's going on in our Lord's heart:

> *Jesus went around to all the towns and villages, teaching in their synagogues, proclaiming the gospel of the kingdom, and curing every disease and illness. At the sight of the crowds, his heart was moved with pity for them because they were troubled and abandoned, like sheep without*

a shepherd. Then he said to his disciples, "The harvest is abundant but the laborers are few; so ask the master of the harvest to send out laborers for his harvest." (Matthew 9:35–38)

Jesus encountered people who felt "troubled and abandoned, like sheep without a shepherd." This is the perennial struggle of the human heart, the reason behind the sincere but often desperate forays of philosophers and religious thinkers of every place and time. The human heart yearns for wisdom and completeness but cannot find it in this fallen world; it yearns to make sense out of life but is stymied at every turn by the paradoxes of evil, suffering, and human misery. Jesus was moved by this human condition, by the angst of the human predicament.

From Worthy Feelings to Effective Action

And what was his reaction? In the very next verses of St. Matthew's Gospel, Jesus called his twelve apostles, gave them a share of his authority and power, and sent them out as his messengers to bring hope, guidance, and healing to all those who are "troubled and abandoned" and otherwise trapped by the forces of evil.

Then he summoned his twelve disciples and gave them authority over unclean spirits to drive them out and to cure every disease and every illness…. Jesus sent out these twelve after instructing them thus, "…As you go, make this proclamation: 'The kingdom of heaven is at hand.' Cure the sick, raise the dead, cleanse lepers, drive out demons…" (Matthew 10:1, 5–8)

Jesus enabled and commanded his followers to do precisely what he had just been doing—preaching, teaching, healing, serving, bringing light into the darkness of needy human hearts. Clearly, the mission of the Church is the outpouring of God's own love for every person.

The commandment "love your neighbor as yourself" should be understood in this context. It embraces much more than a passive avoidance of harm. To love someone, in Christ's mind, is to affirm the goodness of his or her existence and to help that existence flourish. If every Christian is called to participate in the Church's mission of evangelization, it is only because every Christian—and indeed, every human being—is created for love, to be loved, and to love in return. Only this gives our lives the meaning we crave.

Questions for Personal Reflection or Group Discussion

1. What idea in this chapter struck you most and why?

2. Why do you think so many people today consider *obedience* to be a bad word—or at least a bad idea? How would you express in your own words why God wants us to obey his teaching and commandments?

3. What teachings of the Church make you uncomfortable? Which ones do you often feel interior resistance toward? Why? What should you do about that?

4. People can often do the right thing for the wrong reasons. We can do a favor because we want to ask for a favor in return. We can compliment someone because we want to be liked. We can show kindness in order to manipulate. In those cases we are not truly loving the other person—at least, we are not loving that person with a pure heart. This impurity leads to frustration and resentment when we don't get what we want. The path of love that Jesus invites us to follow is different. It seeks to honor the person we are serving, to give of ourselves in a way that will truly help that person, but also respect him or her. This form of love requires more reflection and sensitivity, as well as a denial of our own deep-seated selfish tendencies. But it also creates a climate of interior freedom for us, and an

unambiguous experience of goodness on the part of the one we are serving. Today, how will you seek greater purity of heart in your words and gestures of kindness?

- I will do a hidden act of kindness, something that only God and myself will ever know about.

- I will reflect on situations where I typically end up feeling resentful or frustrated and ask God to show me where those feelings are really rooted.

- I will spend ten minutes today in silent adoration of a crucifix, gazing at Jesus dying on the cross and thinking about the revealed truth that he did it in order to show me how much he loves me.

- (Write your own resolution) I will_____

Concluding Prayer

Jesus, the beginning and fulfillment of the new man, convert our hearts so that, abandoning the ways of error, we may walk in your footsteps on the path which leads to life. Make us live our faith steadfastly, fulfilling our baptismal promises, testifying with conviction to your word, that the life-giving light of the gospel may shine in our families and in society...
Jesus, only-begotten Son of the Father, full of grace and truth, the light which illumines every person, give the abundance of your life to all who seek you with a sincere heart. To you, man's Redeemer, the beginning and the end of time and of the universe, to the Father, unending source of all good, and to the Holy Spirit, seal of infinite love, be all honor and glory, now and for ever. Amen.

—Prayer of St. John Paul II
for the Great Jubilee of the Year 2000

Chapter 6
A New Evangelization?

Over the years, I have often repeated the summons to the new evangelization. I do so again now, especially in order to insist that we must rekindle in ourselves the impetus of the beginnings and allow ourselves to be filled with the ardor of the apostolic preaching which followed Pentecost. We must revive in ourselves the burning conviction of Paul, who cried out: "Woe to me if I do not preach the Gospel" (1 Corinthians 9:16.).

—St. John Paul II, *Novo Millennio Ineunte*, 40

IF EVANGELIZATION IS the deepest identity of the Church, and if the Church has been engaged in evangelization without interruption since the beginning of Christian history, why has the Holy Spirit moved all the postmodern era popes to call so energetically for a "new" evangelization? What does that mean, and what does it have to do with our personal mission as members of the Church?

The Need for Something New

The call for a new evangelization has permeated Church teaching since the mid-twentieth century. The Second Vatican Council, in a sense, set the stage for it. Unlike most ecumenical councils through the ages, this one focused not on clarifying doctrinal issues, but on updating pastoral ones. It was an invitation to reflect on how to make the gospel message resound more effectively in postmodern minds and hearts. St. John XXIII, the pope who called the Council, explained his intentions this way:

Here is the greatest concern of the Ecumenical Council: that the sacred deposit of Christian doctrine should be cared for and taught more and more effectively.... In fact, by opportunely updating herself...the Church will effectively move men, families, and peoples to lift their minds to heavenly things.[8]

Blessed Paul VI, pope for the conclusion of the Council and for the years immediately following it, echoed that same desire for a new energy and effectiveness in evangelization. On the tenth anniversary of the closing of the Second Vatican Council, he published an apostolic exhortation dedicated entirely to evangelization. In it, he explained:

The conditions of the society in which we live oblige all of us therefore to revise methods, to seek by every means to study how we can bring the Christian message to modern man.[9]

---

8 St. John XIII, *Gaudet Mater Ecclesia,* 3, (author's translation). Here is another section from the same discourse that illustrates how this Council was seeking a renewed energy and approach in the Church's age-old evangelizing efforts (emphasis added): "What is needed at the present time is a *new enthusiasm, a new joy and serenity of mind* in the unreserved acceptance by all of the entire Christian faith, without forfeiting that accuracy and precision in its presentation which characterized the proceedings of the Council of Trent and the First Vatican Council. What is needed, and what everyone imbued with a truly Christian, Catholic and apostolic spirit craves today, is that this doctrine shall be *more widely known, more deeply understood, and more penetrating in its effects on men's moral lives.* What is needed is that this certain and immutable doctrine, to which the faithful owe obedience, be *studied afresh and reformulated in contemporary terms.* For this deposit of faith, or truths which are contained in our time-honored teaching is one thing; *the manner in which these truths are set forth* (with their meaning preserved intact) *is something else.* (Wikipedia translation).
9 Blessed Paul VI, *Evangelii Nuntiandi,* 3.

Then he posed three questions at the heart of this call and impulse toward a new evangelization:

In our day, what has happened to that hidden energy of the Good News, which is able to have a powerful effect on man's conscience? To what extent and in what way is that evangelical force capable of really transforming the people of this century? What methods should be followed in order that the power of the gospel may have its effect?[10]

The concept of a new evangelization, therefore, involves recognizing that the world of the third millennium is fundamentally different than the world of previous epochs. Its culture is different. The obstacles and opportunities it offers to the gospel message are different. And so the Church's ongoing work of evangelization must adjust.

The Classic Version: New Ardor, Methods, and Expression

The way St. John Paul II put it has become the classic expression of what the new evangelization really is. In a speech he gave to the bishops of Latin America on the eve of the fifth centenary of the arrival of Christianity to the American continent, he called for a renewed commitment of the Church, a commitment "not of re-evangelization, but rather, of a new evangelization; new in its ardor, methods and expression…"[11] Throughout his quarter-century-long pontificate, St. John Paul II continually reiterated this call to give the ancient thrust of evangelization new forms and new energy.

Naming the New Challenges

Pope Benedict XVI took up the same baton and identified two of the key challenges the new evangelization faces: the globalization

---

10 Ibid., 4.
11 St. John Paul II, Address at the Opening of the 19th Ordinary Plenary Assembly of the Latin American Episcopal Council, 9 March 1983; *L'Osservatore Romano English edition,* 18 April 1983, p. 9.

of a technocratic, secularized mentality and the resultant spiritual numbing of cultures that have had long traditions of vibrant Christian living.

There are regions of the world that are still awaiting a first evangelization; others that have received it, but need a deeper intervention; yet others in which the gospel put down roots a long time ago, giving rise to a true Christian tradition but in which, in recent centuries with complex dynamics the secularization process has produced a serious crisis of the meaning of the Christian faith and of belonging to the Church.[12]

This growing awareness of the need for a new evangelization crystalized in Pope Benedict XVI's erection of a new Pontifical Council explicitly dedicated to promoting it. In its letter of establishment, he mentioned all three cultural climates that the new evangelization must find ways to renew with the gospel message: fervent Christian cultures that need to continue maturing; ancient Christian cultures that have lost their fervor or even rejected completely their former Christian identity and so need to be re-evangelized; and cultures that still have not heard or accepted the gospel and require a newly energized generation of missionaries to reach them.

The secularized, digitalized, global culture of third-millennium humanity does indeed pose unprecedented challenges to evangelization. To make the gospel relevant in this new, "post-Christian" environment may be much more difficult than it was to make the gospel relevant to pre-Christian pagans. Post-Christian people assume that Christianity has been tried and has failed. To evangelize them does indeed require the grace of new, truly inspired "ardor, methods, and expression." Are you ready?

---

12 Pope Benedict XVI, Homily at Vespers, June 28, 2010.

Questions for Personal Reflection or Group Discussion

1. What idea in this chapter struck you most and why?

2. How would you explain the term "new evangelization" to a Catholic friend who hasn't read this chapter?

3. How do you think the immense changes brought to human society by the scientific and technological revolutions of the last couple centuries affect the general tenor of people's religious sensitivity? Imagine if you lived before the invention of electricity. How might that affect the way you see God, humanity, and the world?

4. What are some of the common objections or criticisms you hear applied to Christianity? Where do they come from? How do you usually respond to them? How would you like to be able to respond?

5. The great twentieth-century apologist C.S. Lewis had a personal policy of reading one old book (from a previous period of history) for every four or five contemporary books. He did this because he felt that we all have a tendency to be blind to the errors and prejudices of our own historical epoch. By mixing in books from other epochs, he hoped to keep himself objective about contemporary cultural trends. What will you do today in order to remind yourself that your primary citizenship is in heaven, and that you are only on a passing journey through life on this earth?

- I will visit the grave of a loved one and pray for the repose of his or her soul, maybe bringing flowers for the tombstone.

- I will spend a few hours entirely "unplugged" from technology.

- I will read one of the older papal encyclicals, like Pope Pius XI's *Quas Primas* (Introducing the Feast of Christ the King), St. Pius X's *E Supremi* (On the Restoration of All Things in Christ), or

Blessed Paul VI's apostolic exhortation *Evangelii Nuntiandi* (On Evangelization in the Modern World).

*   (Write your own resolution) I will _____

Concluding Prayer

"Everyone who calls on the name of the Lord will be saved." But how can they call on him in whom they have not believed? And how can they believe in him of whom they have not heard? And how can they hear without someone to preach? And how can people preach unless they are sent? (Romans 10:13–15)

Heavenly Father, pour forth your Holy Spirit to inspire me with these words from Holy Scripture. Stir in my soul the desire to renew my faith and deepen my relationship with your Son, our Lord Jesus Christ, so that I might truly believe in and live the Good News.

Open my heart to hear the Gospel and grant me the confidence to proclaim the Good News to others. Pour out your Spirit, so that I might be strengthened to go forth and witness to the Gospel in my everyday life through my words and actions.

In moments of hesitation, remind me:
If not me, then who will proclaim the Gospel?
If not now, then when will the Gospel be proclaimed?
If not the truth of the Gospel, then what shall I proclaim?

God, our Father, I pray that through the Holy Spirit I might hear the call of the New Evangelization to deepen my faith, grow in confidence to proclaim the Gospel and boldly witness to the saving grace of your Son, Jesus Christ, who lives and reigns with you, in the unity of the Holy Spirit, one God, for ever and ever.
Amen.

—United States Conference of Catholic Bishops,
Prayer for the New Evangelization

Chapter 7
To Teach the Art of Living

Different languages have different words to express what no one would ever wish to lose under any circumstances, what constitutes the expectation, longing and hope of all mankind. But there is no better word than "life" to sum up comprehensively the greatest aspiration of all humanity. "Life" indicates the sum total of all the goods that people desire, and at the same time what makes them possible, obtainable and lasting. Is not the history of mankind deeply marked by a frantic and tragic search for something or someone able to free it from death and guarantee life?... Jesus came to provide the ultimate answer to the yearning for life and for the infinite which his Heavenly Father had poured into our hearts when he created us. At the climax of revelation, the incarnate Word proclaims, "I am the Life" (John 14:6), and "I came that they might have life" (John 10:10). But what life? Jesus' intention was clear: the very life of God, which surpasses all the possible aspirations of the human heart.

—St. John Paul II, Message for the VIII World Youth Day[13]

EVANGELIZATION INVOLVES SPREADING the good news of Jesus Christ and finding ways for his grace and truth to touch, penetrate,

---

13http://w2.vatican.va/content/john-paul-ii/en/messages/youth/documents/hf_jp-ii_mes_15081992_viii-world-youth-day.html.

and transform human hearts, communities, and cultures. The new evangelization strives to do that with new ardor, methods, and expressions.

That's a lot of words and a lot of concepts. What does it all really boil down to? Pope Benedict XVI, before he became pope, summarized it with a beautiful, powerful phrase:

> Our life is an open question, an incomplete project, still to be brought to fruition and realized. Each man's fundamental question is: How will this be realized—becoming man? How does one learn the art of living? Which is the path toward happiness? To evangelize means: to show this path—to teach the art of living.[14]

The Lost Art of Living

The art of living is exactly what was lost by original sin. The human family was created in a condition where our first parents lived in a fruitful and dynamic harmony with the rest of creation, harmony with each other, and harmony with God. That harmony was God's plan for us, and it gave zest and meaning to life.

The great adventure of human existence originally took place in that spiritual arena, when "the Lord God then took the man and settled him in the garden of Eden, to cultivate and care for it" (Genesis 1:28), blessed Adam and Eve, and said to them: "Be fertile and multiply; fill the earth and subdue it" (Genesis 2:15). The happiness we were created to experience was already present from the moment the Lord set the human family on that path. It was a dynamic happiness, meant to grow to fulfillment through loving obedience to God's plan.

Original sin, our first parents' rebellion against God's plan instigated by the deceptions of the devil, shattered that original

---

14 Joseph Cardinal Ratzinger, Address to Catechists and Religion Teachers, Jubilee of Catechists, December 12, 2000. (https://www.ewtn.com/new_evangelization/Ratzinger.htm) (emphasis added).

harmony. Human life became tangled up in confusion and oppressed by misery, as the *Catechism* explains:

> *The harmony in which they had found themselves, thanks to original justice, is now destroyed: the control of the soul's spiritual faculties over the body is shattered; the union of man and woman becomes subject to tensions, their relations henceforth marked by lust and domination. Harmony with creation is broken: visible creation has become alien and hostile to man. Because of man, creation is now subject "to its bondage to decay" (Romans 8:21). Finally, the consequence explicitly foretold for this disobedience will come true: man will "return to the ground" (Genesis 3:19), for out of it he was taken. Death makes its entrance into human history. (CCC, 40)*

Every aspect and sector of human experience suffered the consequences of original sin—and the expanding stain of sin that even today continues to spread out from that epicenter of evil. The human heart still yearns for its original harmony and purpose, but this fallen world frustrates it at every turn. Because of original sin, the original art of living degenerated into a struggle merely to survive and a desperate search for lost meaning.

Recovering the Lost Art of Living

As dire as this situation is, God refused to abandon us. The coming of Jesus, prepared for through God's patient accompaniment and education of the people of Israel, marked the culmination of his plan to restore and even enhance his original design for the human family. To cite Pope Benedict XVI once again:

> *At the beginning of his public life Jesus says: I have come to evangelize the poor (cf. Luke 4:18); this means: I have the response to your fundamental question; I will show*

*you the path of life, the path toward happiness—rather:
I am that path.[15]*

Jesus came to show us how to live and to give us the grace—the divine strength, the forgiveness, the hope, the desire—to live that way. Everything he says and does reveals and enables that fullness of life.

"I am the way and the truth and the life…. I am the light of the world. Whoever follows me will not walk in darkness, but will have the light of life…. I have come that they might have life, and have it more abundantly" (John 14:6, John 8:12, John 10:10).

The essence of evangelization, then, is not complicated. It is as simple as introducing someone to a friend—Jesus. As Jesus's followers and messengers, we don't have all the answers and all the solutions. We too are simply learning the art of living, and that apprenticeship ends only when we die and enter the heavenly kingdom. However much or however little of that art we have learned, though, we can still find ways to share it with others. And when they too meet the Lord, he will take over as their Master, and we will take our proper place as his assistants.

The Benefits of Learning the Art of Living

Simply discovering that the answers to our hearts' deepest questions and longings really do exist begins to spark joy and hope. Simply knowing that there truly is an art of living, a way of living that brings lasting fulfillment, begins to relieve the tense oppression of existential angst and scatter the darkness. Evangelization starts with the announcement that there is an answer, a purpose, and a path, and its name is Jesus. Evangelization moves forward by fostering a deeper and deeper knowledge, love,

15 Ibid.

and following of Jesus. As that increases, the angst and darkness continue to diminish, sin and evil start to lose their grip, and the art of living—along with its resulting experience of joy, hope, and fulfillment—advances.

That's why we say that evangelizing means to teach the art of living, and that's why it is so important.

> *The deepest poverty is the inability of joy, the tediousness of a life considered absurd and contradictory. This poverty is widespread today, in very different forms in the materially rich as well as the poor countries. The inability of joy presupposes and produces the inability to love, produces jealousy, avarice—all defects that devastate the life of individuals and of the world. This is why we are in need of a new evangelization—if the art of living remains an unknown, nothing else works. But this art is not the object of a science—this art can only be communicated by [one] who has life—he who is the Gospel personified.*[16]

The remaining chapters of this book will explore the different ways we can evangelize, and address some obstacles and helps along those ways. But we must never forget the heart of it all: simply saying to others, in whatever language they best understand, *I would love for you to get to know a good friend of mine, who also happens to be the Savior of the world and the King of the universe—his name is Jesus…*

Questions for Personal Reflection or Group Discussion

1. What idea in this chapter struck you most and why?

2. When did you first "meet Jesus"? What led to that moment and what was it like? Remember, savor, and thank God for that experience.

---

16 Ibid.

3. When have you introduced someone to Jesus, knowingly or unknowingly? What led to that moment, and what was it like? What can you learn from that experience?

4. To learn any kind of art is a long and gradual process, and it never really comes to an end. The art of living—the art of being a Christian, knowing, loving, and following Jesus Christ—is no different. We grow in virtue gradually, with plenty of failures. We overcome our sinful habits and tendencies gradually, and sometimes it's painful. Our emotional and spiritual wounds heal gradually under the gentle care of God's grace, often not so quickly as we would like them to. Our understanding of Church teaching deepens gradually, with the aid of study, discussion, and meditation…. If we keep this reality in mind, it helps us avoid the frustration that comes from false expectations. Today, how will you advance and help someone else advance in the art of living?

• I will ask a qualified person (mentor, priest, teacher) to help me better understand a particular Church teaching I have always struggled with.

• I will identify a recurring problem in my life and seek some fresh advice about how better to work on it.

• I will reach out to someone who is suffering and try to be a mirror of God's love for that person.

• (Write your own resolution) I will_____

Concluding Prayer

*It is truly right and just
that we should always give you thanks,
Lord, holy Father, almighty and eternal God.
For you do not cease to spur us on
to possess a more abundant life*

and, being rich in mercy,
you constantly offer pardon
and call on sinners
to trust in your forgiveness alone.
Never did you turn away from us,
and, though time and again we have broken your covenant,
you have bound the human family to yourself
through Jesus your Son, our Redeemer,
with a new bond of love so tight
that it can never be undone.
Even now you set before your people
a time of grace and reconciliation,
and, as they turn back to you in spirit,
you grant them hope in Christ Jesus
and a desire to be of service to all,
while they entrust themselves
more fully to the Holy Spirit.
And so, filled with wonder,
we extol the power of your love,
and, proclaiming our joy
at the salvation that comes from you,
we join in the heavenly hymn of countless hosts,
as without end we acclaim:
Holy, Holy, Holy Lord God of hosts.
Heaven and earth are full of your glory.
Hosanna in the highest.
Blessed is he who comes in the name of the Lord.
Hosanna in the highest.

—*Roman Missal,* Preface for the Eucharist Prayer
for Reconciliation I

Chapter 8
You Are Not Just an Extra Add-On

Pius XII once stated: "The Faithful, more precisely the lay faithful, find themselves on the front lines of the Church's life; for them the Church is the animating principle for human society. Therefore, they in particular, ought to have an ever-clearer consciousness not only of belonging to the Church, but of being the Church, that is to say, the community of the faithful on earth under the leadership of the Pope, the head of all, and of the Bishops in communion with him. These are the Church..."

—St. John Paul II, *Christifedeles Laici*, 9

THE CHURCH HAS a hierarchical structure, established by Christ himself and maintained through more than twenty centuries by the work of the Holy Spirit. Within this hierarchical structure, the ordained clergy act with a sacred power that non-ordained members (the laity) of the Church do not exercise. Christ gives that sacred power, however, for the sake of the whole body of the Church. It is a service—this is the meaning of the word *ministry*. In fact, *ministry* comes from the Latin word *minus*, which literally means "less," in the sense of servants being under those whom they serve.

God Gave Us Shepherds

In the case of the ordained clergy, and in accordance with God's design, their official service is a necessary ingredient in the life of the Church. The *Catechism*, quoting the Second Vatican Council, makes this clear:

> *In order to shepherd the People of God and to increase its numbers without cease, Christ the Lord set up in his Church a variety of offices which aim at the good of the whole body. The holders of office, who are invested with a sacred power, are, in fact, dedicated to promoting the interests of their brethren, so that all who belong to the People of God…may attain to salvation. (CCC, 874)*

Thus the hierarchy of the Church, the pope and the bishops along with their collaborators, the priests and deacons, provides the sacramental and magisterial (i.e., dependable teaching) fonts by which the whole Mystical Body of Christ continues to be nourished and strengthened.

No Second-Class Citizens

And yet the critical nature of that office and the sacred authority that goes with it do not relegate lay members of the Church to a kind of second-class status. Lay members are not meant to be merely passive collaborators with the ordained clergy. When laypersons think in those terms, they handcuff their evangelizing potential.

The essential identity of the Church is found in its evangelizing mission, as we have seen, and in that mission the laity have a dignity and responsibility as real and substantial as the ordained clergy. Here is how the *Catechism* puts it:

> *In virtue of their rebirth in Christ there exists among all the Christian faithful a true equality with regard to dignity and the activity whereby all cooperate in the building up of the Body of Christ in accord with each one's own condition and function. (CCC, 872)*

In other words, God has designed the Church in such a way that her mission of evangelizing the world and building up his Mystical Body requires a dual fidelity: ordained ministers must be faithful to their official service, and lay members must be faithful to their identity and mission. The hierarchy cannot sanctify the world without the laity, and the laity cannot sanctify the world without the hierarchy. Lay members are not mere extras or hangers-on; they have real responsibility for the life and work of the Church.

A Change in Mentality

Pope Benedict XVI stressed this aspect of dynamic communion between the hierarchy and the laity in a message to Catholic Action, one of the first lay movements in the modern Church. To describe it he focused on the operative term "co-responsibility":

> *Co-responsibility requires a change in mentality, particularly with regard to the role of the laity in the Church, who should be considered not as "collaborators" with the clergy, but as persons truly "co-responsible" for the being and activity of the Church.*[17]

The mentality of co-responsibility implies that lay members of the Church should feel the mission of the Church as their own, whether they are consecrated or non-consecrated laypeople. The laity should feel empowered by their baptism to engage fully in the Church's life and mission, being proactive and not only reactive evangelizers. And the ordained ministers should recognize and respect the spirit of initiative that goes along with this co-responsibility.

Complementary Spheres

The primary sphere of this lay activity of the Church differs from the

---

17 Benedict XVI, Message for the International Forum of Catholic Action, August 10, 2012; http://w2.vatican.va/content/benedict-xvi/en/messages/pont-messages/2012/documents/hf_ben-xvi_mes_20120810_fiac.html.

primary sphere of the activity of the ordained ministers. The clergy are first and foremost ministers of the Word and the sacraments, as well as of the internal governance of the People of God required for those ministries to be effective. Laypersons, on the other hand, are first and foremost messengers of Christ into the secular world, and the Church needs them to evangelize proactively there, to take the initiative in Christianizing (or re-Christianizing) culture:

> *By reason of their special vocation it belongs to the laity to seek the kingdom of God by engaging in temporal affairs and directing them according to God's will…. The initiative of lay Christians is necessary especially when the matter involves discovering or inventing the means for permeating social, political, and economic realities with the demands of Christian doctrine and life. This initiative is a normal element of the life of the Church… (CCC, 898, 899)*

This doesn't mean that laypeople should never be allowed in the sacristy and priests should never be allowed out of the sacristy. That would be a distorted exaggeration, undermining communion rather than fostering it. But it does mean that the co-responsibility envisioned by the Lord for the Church involves a deep and real complementarity of roles between clergy and laity.

A Dynamic and Determined Communion

If clergy view their own ministry as essential to the Church while viewing an active and engaged laity as a nice extra, or add-on, their service to laypersons will be seriously debilitated. Likewise, if the laity ignores or overrides the sacred power granted to clergy, lay members will thwart the advance of Christ's kingdom.

But the contrary is equally true. If clergy belittle and neglect their ecclesial ministry, the people they serve will become spiritually anemic. And if the laity passively sit around in the pews and wait for "the Church" to do something about the social and cultural realities that need to be evangelized, evil will continue to advance.

We all need to recognize that the critical mission of evangelization requires a Church living in dynamic communion, with clergy and laity creatively working together, each ardently and doggedly engaged in their common mission according to their own roles and gifts.

Questions for Personal Reflection or Group Discussion

1. What idea in this chapter struck you most and why?

2. How would you explain in your own words the concept of ecclesial co-responsibility? In order to understand it more deeply, think of specific examples from your own experience in the Church when that co-responsibility has been lived poorly or especially well.

3. How well do your attitudes toward the clergy and laity you know reflect the dynamic communion that we are all called to live?

4. In the message where Pope Benedict XVI utilized the term "co-responsibility," he gave some advice to the lay members of the Church: "May you feel as your own the commitment to working for the Church's mission: with prayers, study and active participation in ecclesial life, with an attentive and positive gaze at the world, in the constant search for the signs of the times. Through a serious and daily commitment to formation never tire of increasingly refining the aspects of your specific vocation as lay faithful called to be courageous and credible witnesses in all social milieus so that the gospel may be a light that brings hope to the problematic, difficult and dark situations which people today often encounter in their journey through life." What will you do today to follow that sound advice?

•   I will jumpstart my prayer life by reviewing and renewing my daily and weekly prayer commitments, making sure they are substantial but also realistic.

- I will take some time to write down what being a "courageous and credible witness" of the gospel could look like in the milieus of my life.
- I will sign up for a spiritual retreat or pilgrimage as a way to deepen my own Christian formation.
- (Write your own resolution) I will_____

Concluding Prayer

*Lord, renew your Church
by the light of the Gospel.
Strengthen the bond of unity
between the faithful and the pastors of your people,
together with our Pope, our Bishop,
and the whole Order of Bishops,
that in a world torn by strife
your people may shine forth
as a prophetic sign of unity and concord.
Remember our brothers and sisters
who have fallen asleep in the peace of your Christ,
and all the dead, whose faith you alone have known.
Admit them to rejoice in the light of your face,
and in the resurrection give them the fullness of life.
Grant also to us, when our earthly pilgrimage is done,
that we may come to an eternal dwelling place
and live with you for ever;
there, in communion with the Blessed Virgin Mary, Mother of God,
with the Apostles and Martyrs,
and with all the Saints,
we shall praise and exalt you
through Jesus Christ, your Son. Amen.*

—*Roman Missal,* from the Eucharistic Prayer for Use
in Masses for Various Needs I

PART II
Things to Keep in Mind

After this the Lord appointed seventy-two others whom he sent ahead of him in pairs to every town and place he intended to visit. He said to them, "The harvest is abundant but the laborers are few; so ask the master of the harvest to send out laborers for his harvest.
—Luke 10:1–2

Chapter 9
You Have What It Takes

*Christ's gift of the Holy Spirit is going to be poured out upon you
in a particular way. You will hear the words of the Church spoken
over you, calling upon the Holy Spirit to confirm your faith, to seal
you in his love, to strengthen you for his service. You will then take
your place among fellow-Christians throughout the world, full
citizens now of the People of God. You will witness to the truth of
the gospel in the name of Jesus Christ. You will live your lives in
such a way as to make holy all human life. Together with all the
confirmed you will become living stones in the cathedral of peace.
Indeed you are called by God to be instruments of his peace.*

—St. John Paul II, Homily for Pentecost, May 30, 1982

THE CHURCH'S DEEPEST identity is found in her mission to
evangelize, to proclaim and foster the growth of Christ's kingdom.
And God calls every Christian, every member of the Church, no
matter how apparently small or unqualified, to join in that mission
and make a unique, unrepeatable contribution to it that will
reverberate throughout eternity. Making that contribution is every
Christian's best way to "love your neighbor as yourself."

This mission can make us feel excited. But it can also make
us feel scared, intimidated, and inadequate. You might think,
*The great saints were capable of something like that, something so
transcendental and amazing, but that's not for me. I can barely keep*

myself together in the hustle and bustle of daily duties and never-ending mini-crises! Who am I to think that I can help build Christ's kingdom and love like that?

Feelings Bolstered by Faith

It's understandable to feel that way. But sometimes our spontaneous feelings only give us a partial glimpse into reality, especially in the realm of faith. Feelings need to be educated, taught to incorporate the truths of our faith into all the information they process and communicate to us. And on this point, about the capacity of every Christian to become a saint and make a unique, unrepeatable contribution to Christ's kingdom, our faith rescues us from every feeling of fear or inadequacy, for one simple reason: Our efforts are not just *our* efforts.

Naturally, depending only on hard work and our own natural powers and gifts, the call to holiness and evangelization is indeed far beyond our capacities. Christ's kingdom, as we have seen, "does not belong to this world" (John 18:36). It is a supernatural kingdom, built up by the power of grace and the Holy Spirit. If we were to try to take our place in that kingdom by leaning solely on our earthly smarts and strengths, we would be perennially frustrated, fruitlessly aiming again and again and again at a target impossibly beyond our reach.

New Things Have Come

But part of the good news Jesus brings is that, through baptism and confirmation, our natural gifts and talents—however many or few they may be—are healed and enhanced by grace. They are plugged in to the divine life itself. Baptism makes us adopted children of God, not just as some kind of formality, but in truth. Anyone who is baptized has "come to share in the divine nature…. So whoever is in Christ is a new creation: the old things have passed away; behold, new things have come" (2 Peter 1:4, 2 Corinthians 5:17).

We are members of Christ's own body, and through the sacrament of confirmation, the same Holy Spirit that animates Christ and the Church has been abundantly poured into our own lives, animating each one of us as well: "Now you are Christ's body, and individually parts of it…hope does not disappoint, because the love of God has been poured out into our hearts through the holy Spirit that has been given to us…" (1 Corinthians 12:27, Romans 5:5). And so our human and material limitations, our wounds, our struggles and hardships—none of these things have to inhibit us from engaging in this uniquely fulfilling mission of evangelization. God can work through them all, and when we let him do so, he is glorified even more than when we try to serve him from a place of self-satisfaction and self-confidence.

When We Are Weak, We Are Strong

St. Paul learned this lesson the hard way—through a mysterious struggle against what he calls "a thorn in the flesh" that he simply could never get rid of:

> *Therefore, that I might not become too elated, a thorn in the flesh was given to me, an angel of Satan, to beat me, to keep me from being too elated. Three times I begged the Lord about this, that it might leave me, but he said to me, "My grace is sufficient for you, for power is made perfect in weakness." I will rather boast most gladly of my weaknesses, in order that the power of Christ may dwell with me. Therefore, I am content with weaknesses, insults, hardships, persecutions, and constraints, for the sake of Christ; for when I am weak, then I am strong. (2 Corinthians 12:7–10, emphasis added)*

The same Holy Spirit that comes to us through the grace of baptism and confirmation, truly uniting us to God and gradually leading us to spiritual maturity, also equips us and spurs us on toward the fulfillment of our mission in Christ's kingdom. Some Christians are called to carry out dramatic and highly visible missions, like St. Bernadine of Siena, who would habitually preach to crowds of 10,000 people. Others are called to carry out hidden but still beautiful and powerful missions, like St. Joseph, who silently cared for Jesus and Mary, without speaking even a single word in the Bible.

You Are Not Lacking

Whatever he may ask of each one of us, "God is faithful," and through Christ he doesn't call and equip us for something beyond our reach—that would be torture. Rather:

> …in him you were enriched in every way, with all discourse and all knowledge…so that you are not lacking in any spiritual gift as you wait for the revelation of our Lord Jesus Christ. He will keep you firm to the end, irreproachable on the day of our Lord Jesus [Christ]. (1 Corinthians 1:9, 5–8)

When Jesus sent his twelve apostles out on their first mission, St. Matthew tells us that he "summoned his twelve disciples and *gave them authority*…" (Matthew 10:1, emphasis added). When he sent the larger group of seventy-two followers, St. Luke tells us that "the Lord *appointed*" them (Luke 10:1, emphasis added). At his ascension, Jesus prefaces his great commission that the Church "go, therefore, and make disciples of all nations" with an explanation of whose power will truly be at work within the Church's efforts to fulfill that command: "Then Jesus approached and said to them, 'All power in heaven and on earth has been given to me. Go, therefore…'" (Matthew 28:18–19).

As Christians, through the mysterious communion with God given by baptism and confirmation, Christ's own life surges through our veins. His own power gives supernatural force to our evangelizing efforts. Insofar as we intentionally and consistently nourish this communion through a growing prayer life, through a humble and determined participation in the Eucharist and in confession, and through a decent effort to obey the Lord's will in all things, it will mature and expand, bringing God's unique dream for each one of us to fulfillment.[18]

Truly, your part in building up Christ's kingdom is beyond anything you could ever do—on your own. But in the Lord, you really do have what it takes.

Questions for Personal Reflection or Group Discussion

1. What idea in this chapter struck you most and why?

2. When you think about the sacrament of baptism, what comes to mind? Why? Why do you think we celebrate our birthdays, but not many of us celebrate the anniversary of our baptism?

3. When you think of the sacrament of confirmation, what comes to mind? Why? Remember your own experience of receiving this sacrament. What sticks in your mind? Why? What would you like to have done differently?

4. The life of grace within us is invisible and most often works in hidden ways, like all the seeds that Jesus refers to in his parables about his kingdom. And yet grace is real, and it has produced and inspired all the works of the Church throughout its history: the spiritual maturity, power, and influence of the saints, and the countless acts of mercy, self-sacrifice, fidelity, and kindness performed by thousands and thousands of Christian lives through the centuries. What will you do today to allow God's grace to flow freely in and through your life?

---

18 Those are essential aspects of our Christian discipleship, and they were treated in greater detail in the author's two previous works: *The Better Part: A Christ-Centered Resource for Personal Prayer* and *Seeking First the Kingdom: 30 Meditations on How to Love God with All Your Heart, Soul, Mind, and Strength.*

- I will find out the baptismal anniversaries of every member of my family (including my own) and plan to celebrate them with the same gusto that we celebrate our birthdays.

- I will take some time to read up on the life of the saint whose name I took when I was confirmed in order to derive some fresh inspiration from how grace worked in his or her life.

- I will renew my commitment to spending some time (fifteen minutes, for example) in personal prayer with the Lord every single day in order to keep his grace flowing in my mind and heart.

- (Write your own resolution) I will_____

Concluding Prayer

O God, whose ancient wonders
remain undimmed in splendor even in our day,
for what you once bestowed on a single people,
freeing them from Pharaoh's persecution
by the power of your right hand
now you bring about as the salvation of the nations
through the waters of rebirth,
grant, we pray, that the whole world
may become children of Abraham
and inherit the dignity of Israel's birthright.
Through Christ our Lord. Amen.

—*Roman Missal,* Prayer after the Third Reading
for the Easter Vigil Mass

Chapter 10
The Gifts You May Not
Even Know You Have

*In our own day, too, the Spirit is the principal agent of the
new evangelization. Hence it will be important to gain a
renewed appreciation of the Spirit as the One who builds the
Kingdom of God within the course of history and prepares its
full manifestation in Jesus Christ, stirring people's hearts and
quickening in our world the seeds of the full salvation which will
come at the end of time.*

—St. John Paul II, *Tertio Millennio Adveniente,* 45

THE DIVINE LIFE that makes us children of God and equips us
to make our unique contribution to the Church's mission of
evangelization works in many and mysterious ways. Through the
centuries, the Church has gradually come to understand partially
and even categorize some of them. Dedicating some time to reflect
on this knowledge can bolster our confidence in God. It can also
prepare us to grasp the many different (and sometimes surprising)
forms that our evangelizing mission can take in the midst of our
daily lives.

When the life of grace takes root in us, it grafts onto the natural
powers of our souls the supernatural gifts of the Holy Spirit. By
doing this, God doesn't override our personalities and use us as

some kind of robot-slaves to build up his kingdom. But he does equip us with all we need to live our missionary vocation to the fullest. Our potential to develop natural virtues and reach human maturity is enhanced, so we can also truly develop supernatural virtues (sometimes referred to as *infused* virtues) and reach full Christian maturity—the holiness that brings lasting happiness.

Wisdom from Narnia

C.S. Lewis communicated this relationship between natural and supernatural powers beautifully, though poetically, in his delightful classic, *The Lion, the Witch and the Wardrobe.*

As the four children from earth make their way through the magical realm of Narnia, which has long been suffering under the curse of an evil witch, they run across Santa Claus. In this strange encounter, jolly Father Christmas gives each of the children a special gift—a sword for Peter, a vial of healing potion for Lucy, and so on. As the story unfolds and the four children engage in their mission to liberate Narnia from its curse, each one of the gifts is used in critical moments. Those gifts didn't take the place of each child's natural personality, with its natural strengths and weaknesses, but rather the gifts were customized in order to allow each child's personality to flourish and expand beyond what he or she could have imagined.

Ordinary and Extraordinary Gifts

It is likewise with God's grace in our lives. It equips our natural human powers with the seven universal gifts of the Holy Spirit (which every Christian receives; that why we can call them "universal") and an assortment of other, charismatic gifts as well (distributed only to specific individuals in accordance with God's providence).

Four of the seven universal gifts heal and enhance our mental powers. Through the *gift of wisdom*, the Holy Spirit opens our minds to know about God—not only from a distance, so to speak, but to know God himself directly—to taste the divine goodness itself. This is considered the highest gift, because this experience unfailingly deepens and confirms the soul's union with God.

The second gift that renews our mind in Christ is the *gift of understanding*. This enables us to grasp the truths that God has revealed to us about himself and about our salvation; it gives us the ability to penetrate their depths and see more clearly how they relate to one another. The third gift, the *gift of knowledge*, is similar. It enables us to view and interpret normal human events and earthly realities as God does—in light of eternal truths. The fourth gift, the *gift of counsel*, builds on the third. If the gift of knowledge helps us see ordinary human events and earthly realities from God's perspective, the gift of counsel helps us navigate the extraordinary ones, guiding us when the right course of action is hard to fathom.

The remaining three universal gifts heal and strengthen the powers related to our will, our capacity to make free choices. The first of these, the *gift of piety*, gives us a supernatural affection for God as our loving Father and for other people as brothers and sisters in God's family. In other words, piety fuels a desire to live in a faith-based communion of hearts with God and with others.

If the gift of piety gives us supernatural affections, the next gift, the *gift of fortitude*, gives us supernatural strength in the face of spiritual obstacles and enemies.

The third gift that the Holy Spirit uses to heal our fallen freedom is the *gift of holy fear*, what the Bible calls the "fear of the Lord" (Proverbs 9:10). This isn't a slavish fear of punishment, but a filial fear of being separated from God, like an interior warning alarm that goes off when we find ourselves in morally and spiritually dangerous situations. It helps us turn around, flee, or change course, so that we avoid the threat altogether.

These seven universal or ordinary gifts can be referred to as Christological gifts, because God gives them to every Christian in order to help each of us live more and more as Christ lived, so we can continue his mission on earth.

The Bible and our theological tradition also identify other gifts from the Holy Spirit, sometimes called the charismatic gifts. They can also be called extraordinary gifts, because they are not ordinarily given to every Christian. These include prophecy, special discernment of spirits, healing, and miracles. In contrast to the Christological gifts, these can be understood as ecclesiastical gifts, because they are always given for the sake of building up the community of believers, the Church. They do not necessarily help the person who receives them become holy.

Beyond Feelings

You may feel like the gifts of the Holy Spirit aren't present in your soul, but as long as you are living a life of grace, they are. As your relationship with Christ deepens, as you love him more and more with all your heart, soul, mind, and strength, the gifts work more and more freely. In that way, you become more docile to the Holy Spirit, "the One who builds the kingdom of God within the course of history," as St. John Paul II put it. And increased docility to the Holy Spirit means that God's dream for your life and your unique mission in the Church unfold and flourish more fully, regardless of how palpably you feel it. After all, in Christ's parable about the Last Judgment, many of those who were rewarded for their service to Jesus were surprised to discover that their normal behavior had actually contributed to building up Christ's kingdom; the truth of that eternal kingdom often transcends our temporal awareness (see Matthew 25:31–46).

Questions for Personal Reflection or Group Discussion

1. What idea in this chapter struck you most and why?

2. Which of the seven universal gifts of the Holy Spirit do you think would be most helpful for your life right now and why?

Ask the Lord to increase that gift in your soul and enable you to make use of it.

3. The charismatic gifts are spoken about much more frequently than the Christological gifts. Why do you think that is? How do you think the devil feels about that discrepancy, and why?

4. The gifts are present in our souls, but in order for them to flourish we have to cooperate with them. This cooperation can take many forms, including *feeding holy desires and accepting holy inspirations*. A holy desire is a desire for the things that make us holy—living closer to God, being more like Christ (courageous, humble, loving, wise…), finding and fulfilling our life's vocation. Most of us do desire these things deep down. But more mundane desires seem to occupy our attention more regularly: We think about making more money, feeling more relaxed, climbing social or professional ladders, finding more ways to enjoy ourselves…. These natural desires aren't evil, but unless we intentionally feed the holier ones, the natural ones will monopolize our attention and make it harder for us to follow where God wants to lead us. Accepting holy inspiration is another way to cooperate with the Holy Spirit's gifts. God is always nudging us toward actions and decisions that will build up his kingdom in our hearts and in the hearts of those around us. He give us little inspirations, gentle whispers that we hear in the depth of our hearts: *Call that person today; go and visit that person; take some time to pray before you go to work; take some more time to listen.* Often these inspirations aren't attractive on the surface, because they require some self-sacrifice. But if we train ourselves to listen to them and heed them, we give God more room to work in our lives, and our spiritual growth accelerates. What will you do today to feed holy desires and accept holy invitations?

• I will make time to read that spiritual book I have been wanting to read for a long time.

- I will reach out to that person I know I should have reached out to already but haven't gotten around to.

- I will take inventory of the kind of media products I watch and listen to and eliminate one or two that consistently have a bad effect on me.

- (Write your own resolution) I will_____

Concluding Prayer

Confirm, O God,
what you have brought about in us,
and preserve in the hearts of your faithful
the gifts of the Holy Spirit:
may they never be ashamed
to confess Christ crucified before the world
and by devoted charity
may they ever fulfill his commands.
Instruct, O Lord, in the fullness of the Law
those you have endowed with the gifts of your Spirit
and nourished by the Body of your Only Begotten Son,
that they may constantly show to the world
the freedom of your adopted children
and, by the holiness of their lives,
exercise the prophetic mission of your people.
Through Christ our Lord. Amen.

—*Roman Missal,* Prayer Over the People from the Mass for the Conferral of Confirmation, A and B

Chapter 11
Is Self-Love Good or Bad?

Man as "willed" by God, as "chosen" by him from eternity and called, destined for grace and glory—this is "each" man, "the most concrete" man, "the most real"; this is man in all the fullness of the mystery in which he has become a sharer in Jesus Christ, the mystery in which each one of the four thousand million human beings living on our planet has become a sharer from the moment he is conceived beneath the heart of his mother.

—St. John Paul II, *Redemptor Hominis,* 13

IN THE SECOND of the two great commandments, Jesus tells us to "love your neighbor as yourself" (Matthew 22:39). Yet later on, in the Gospel of John, Jesus affirms that "Whoever loves his life loses it, and whoever hates his life in this world will preserve it for eternal life" (John 12:25). St. Matthew also records that saying, but with a slight variation: "Whoever finds his life will lose it, and whoever loses his life for my sake will find it" (Matthew 10:39).

Two Brands of Self-Love

Is Jesus contradicting himself? On the one hand, he assumes that we love ourselves enough to be able to use self-love as a standard for how to treat our neighbor. On the other hand, he warns us against loving our lives, as if doing so will lead to self-destruction. How are we to understand this? Untangling this knot matters, because without doing so we can't really open the door to the realm of loving our neighbor as Jesus wants us to.

Traditional Christian spirituality identifies two brands of self-love, a healthy one and an unhealthy one. Healthy self-love sees and accepts oneself as created good by God, loved by him personally and unconditionally, appreciated and valued and affirmed by a heavenly Father who loved us so much that "he gave his only Son, so that everyone who believes in him might not perish but might have eternal life…. See what love the Father has bestowed on us that we may be called the children of God. Yet so we are" (John 3:16; 1 John 3:1).

Gradually coming to recognize this love that God has for us and accept it wholeheartedly constitutes one of the main dynamisms of spiritual growth. Our fallen nature tends to resist this love, mainly because it is unconditional and therefore outside of our control, but also because we have often been wounded and told that we are unlovable. Our tendency toward pride and self-sufficiency, exacerbated by those wounds, fears what is beyond our control. And so that fallen, broken part of us prefers to earn love, to try and make ourselves lovable through actions and accomplishments. It's hard for us to accept the revealed truth that, from God's perspective, nothing we can do will increase of decrease his love for us. He loves us fully already, because of who we are, not because of what we do or don't do.

Why Healthy Self-Love Is Healthy

As we learn to accept God's love for us, we also learn to love ourselves in a healthy way—not because we are better than other people; not because we have made ourselves so excellent; but simply because we are created in God's image and he rejoices in us: "For the Lord takes delight in his people" (Psalm 149:4). We learn to appreciate and even look with awe at the amazing dignity we have been given, not through any merit of our own, but simply through God's overflowing goodness: "I praise you, because I am wonderfully made; wonderful are your works!" (Psalm 139:14).

The awareness of ourselves as beloved by God nourishes humility and opens our souls to his grace. In so doing it fosters all the other virtues as well, giving us deeper reserves of strength and clearer motives to act in accordance with our true dignity—to be just, and temperate, and courageous, and prudent. This is healthy self-love, a self-love that flows from God and carries us toward God.

Simple Selfishness

Unhealthy self-love is what spiritual writers call *disordered* self-love, an exaggerated and distorted view of one's goodness, as if it were existentially independent and the central value of the entire universe.

This brand of self-love is nothing more than self-centeredness, egoism, and self-absorption. It is an interior twistedness inherited from original sin and exacerbated by personal sin and the sinful trends present in many of human society's norms and customs. This kind of self-love sees all things as revolving around oneself, and it idolizes self to the point of seeking self-aggrandizement above anything else. Other people become merely obstacles or tools. God does, too. Life in this world is lived in terms of exalting one's self-image at any price. Happiness is pursued not through loving God and neighbor, but through feeding one's ego by acquiring more and more pleasure, popularity, or power—the focal points of the false promises of a fallen world. It distorts our true identity, the way Gollum's obsession with the Ring of Power twisted and distorted him into a shadow of his true self in Tolkien's *Lord of the Rings*. Disordered self-love is the Gollum syndrome.

A Challenge for Everyone

Selfishness may seem extreme and rare when described so starkly.

And yet we all have a built-in tendency to live that way. Every sin is an effervescence of that tendency, a victory of what St. Paul calls the "old self":

You should put away the old self of your former way of life, corrupted through deceitful desires, and be renewed in the spirit of your minds, and put on the new self, created in God's way in righteousness and holiness of truth. (Ephesians 4:22–24)

When Jesus warns us that "Whoever loves his life loses it, and whoever hates his life in this world will preserve it for eternal life" (John 12:25), he is evoking this Pauline contrast and admonishing us to avoid unhealthy self-love. He wants us to center our desires on God and his will, rather than on the idols of the world—which, as Pope Francis reminded us in his first encyclical letter, "exist, we begin to see, as a pretext for setting ourselves at the center of reality and worshiping the work of our own hands."[19]

On the other hand, when Jesus commands us to "love your neighbor as your self," he is evoking healthy self-love as the core criterion for attitudes and behaviors toward others. The same criterion undergirds the earlier Gospel expression of the Golden Rule: "Do to others whatever you would have them do to you. This is the law and the prophets" (Matthew 7:12).

Loving Your Neighbor as Yourself

Even before we reach spiritual maturity, our deeper self (as opposed to our derivative, fallen nature) instinctually—and rightly—values and prefers things that help us live life well to things that harm and disorient us. When we are in need, we hope to find assistance. When we make mistakes, we hope to be given a second chance. When we are confused, we hope to be enlightened. Those are legitimate hopes, because assistance and second chances and

---

19 Pope Francis, *Lumen Fidei*, 13.

enlightenment are all directed toward the full flourishing of a person created, redeemed, and unconditionally loved by God.

That full flourishing is a good thing; it is the object of a healthy self-love and the reason why sensible self-care glorifies God. And just as we spontaneously desire and pursue those legitimate hopes for ourselves, true love—the generous, Christ-like, Trinitarian love whose image and likeness constitutes our deepest identity and therefore our most authentic happiness—moves us to desire them and also pursue them for our neighbor.

This is why, as we shall see, evangelization includes not just preaching and praying, but also every good deed within our reach.

Questions for Personal Reflection or Group Discussion

1. What idea in this chapter struck you most and why?

2. How would you describe in your own words the difference between healthy and unhealthy self-love?

3. When have you been the recipient of the love-for-neighbor Jesus commands of us? How did it make you feel and why?

4. Because healthy self-love flows from seeing oneself as God does, it educates us about how to see others, too. God loves us and showers us with his gifts even though we are riddled with flaws, wounds, and sinful tendencies. God loves us in a way that never stops affirming the sinner even while condemning the sin. God never gives up on us, even when there seems to be little hope for improvement: "If we are unfaithful he remains faithful, for he cannot deny himself" (2 Timothy 2:13). What will you do today to learn better how to see yourself and others as God does?

• I will spend some time today looking at a crucifix and reflecting on the fact that Jesus died for me—to pay the price for my sins, to show me the depths of his love, and to open for me the gates of heaven.

- I will pay special attention today to the needs of those around me and make an effort to meet them whenever I can.

- I will speak a little bit less and listen a little bit more in all my conversations today, to help avoid falling into self-centeredness.

- (Write your own resolution) I will_____.

Concluding Prayer

*O God, who have taught your Church
to keep all the heavenly commandments
by loving you and loving our neighbor,
grant us a spirit of peace and grace,
so that your entire family
may be devoted to you wholeheartedly
and united in purity of intent.
Through our Lord Jesus Christ, your Son,
who lives and reigns with you in the unity of the Holy Spirit,
one God, for ever and ever. Amen.*

—*Roman Missal,* Second Collect for the Mass
for Promoting Harmony

Chapter 12
Where to Start?

To all who are listening to my voice I wish to say that the age of the missions is not over; Christ still needs generous men and women to become heralds of the Good News to the ends of the earth. Do not be afraid to follow him. Share freely with others the faith you have received! No believer in Christ, no institution of the Church can avoid this supreme duty: to proclaim Christ to all peoples.

—St. John Paul II, Homily in Gambia, February 23, 1992;
Redemptoris Missio, 3

WE ALL REMEMBER the Gospel passages where Jesus multiplies the loaves. On one occasion he fed more than five thousand people with only five loaves of bread and two dried fish (see Matthew 14:13–21). On another occasion he fed more than four thousand people with only seven loaves of bread and a few fish (see Matthew 15:32–39).

Does God Ask the Impossible?

In both cases it seemed to Christ's apostles that he was asking them something impossible. He longed to feed the hungry crowds who were following him:

"My heart is moved with pity for the crowd, for they have been with me now for three days and have nothing to eat.

I do not want to send them away hungry, for fear they may collapse on the way." (Matthew 15:32)

But the little group of chosen apostles was more practical. "The disciples said to him, 'Where could we ever get enough bread in this deserted place to satisfy such a crowd?'" (Matthew 15:33).

On the first occasion of this miracle, the apostles actually advised Jesus to simply send the crowds away to fend for themselves. It's an understandable reaction. But Jesus turned and looked them in the eye and said: "There is no need for them to go away; give them some food yourselves" (Matthew 14:16). He was not stupid. He knew the scanty resources at their disposal. "But they said to him, 'Five loaves and two fish are all we have here'" (Matthew 14:17). They really did have very little. Their merely natural possibilities to achieve what Jesus was asking them to do were ridiculously inadequate.

Feeling Overwhelmed

Most of us can identify with that, if we are honest. The moral demands of our faith overwhelm us—it seems impossible to live the life of patience, purity, generosity, and courage we know we are called to live. The apostolic demands of being a Christian missionary weigh us down; we find ourselves barely able to fulfill the basic duties of everyday life, let alone branch out into creative ways to evangelize the world—even if we could think of some.

Truly, we find ourselves looking at Jesus with the same pained—and maybe even frustrated or resentful—expression of the disciples in the Gospel: "Five loaves and two fish are all that we have here." *Lord, I just don't have the strength, the time, the knowledge to do this. If I give away the little I have, I don't think I will be able to survive. I really need those few loaves and fish. I can't help you—I can barely help myself…*

Jesus Knows Our Limitations

Jesus understands that. In fact, he knows our limitations better than we know them ourselves. When St. John told his version of the multiplication of the loaves, he points this out explicitly, even with a bit of humor.

> *When Jesus raised his eyes and saw that a large crowd was coming to him, he said to Philip, "Where can we buy enough food for them to eat?" He said this to test him, because he himself knew what he was going to do. (John 6:5–6)*

Jesus knows our limitations. He knows that by our own power the Christian life he invites us to live is a mere pipedream. But at the same time, he doesn't share those limitations. He is God. His grace can radically transform and multiply the slightest and most paltry effort to build his kingdom, to love our neighbors, just as his grace transformed the few loaves and fish into an abundant feast. He just needs us to do one thing, one little thing, to make that happen. "Then he said, 'Bring them here to me'" (Matthew 14:18).

Jesus Works Within Our Limitations

When the apostles placed their meager resources into the Lord's hands, they didn't know what would happen. All they knew was that Jesus could be trusted. Jesus would take care of it. Jesus would find a way to make it work out. Jesus would not waste even a crumb of whatever they put into his hands and offered to him for the advance of his kingdom. Not even a crumb. In fact, after the miracle was over and Jesus had fed thousands with the little his disciples had given him, he still wasn't finished.

> *…[H]e said to his disciples, "Gather the fragments left over, so that nothing will be wasted." So they collected them, and filled twelve wicker baskets with fragments from the*

five barley loaves that had been more than they could eat.
(John 6:12–13)

This is how it works with the Lord. The gifts he gives us, the gifts of grace and the Holy Spirit, miraculously multiply our slightest effort to live as Christ asks us to live. In order to fulfill our Christian mission in the world, we don't have to have a perfect master plan or a fail-safe formula. All we have to do is offer what we have and let Jesus multiply it. We just have to give to others what Jesus has given to us—a few loaves of faith and a couple words of hope— and he will do the rest. That's the way to start. That's how the Lord wants us to start: leaning not on our natural smarts and strengths, but stepping out of our comfort zone and leaning on him.

From Plain Bread to Holy Host

This whole dynamism is beautifully present every time we go to Mass. We offer to God the humble gifts of bread and wine— the most normal, earthly products of nature and human labor. We place them on the altar, in all their plainness, simplicity, and fragility. And what happens? They become hosts of Christ's own precious Body and Blood. God "gracifies" them, transforming them into something that no human effort, however magnificent, could ever accomplish: the Eucharistic presence of the Lord himself.

Lord, I only have five loaves and two fish, how can I help build your kingdom?

"Bring them here to me…"

Questions for Personal Reflection or Group Discussion

1. What idea in this chapter struck you most and why?

2. When have you experienced the power of God's grace transforming your limited efforts into a true advance for

his kingdom? Remember, savor, and thank him for those experiences.

3. What are the loaves and fish available to you personally, and how is God asking you to put them at the service of his kingdom?

4. Why do you think God sometimes asks us to do more than we are naturally capable of?

5. A famous story about St. Francis of Assisi illustrates this point. St. Francis was the founder of the Franciscan Order, which has been one of the Church's most fruitful spiritual and missionary powerhouses ever since its foundation in the high Middle Ages. But Francis didn't start off with that in mind. He just wanted to serve the Lord. One day early on in his faith journey, he was praying in front of a crucifix in the church of San Damiano, just outside the walls of Assisi, a small city in the Italian region of Umbria. As he prayed, our Lord appeared to him, and the crucifix spoke to him, saying "Francis, rebuild my church." The Lord was calling him to his great work of founding the Franciscan Order, an army of Christians dedicated to reform and renewal. But Francis didn't understand that yet. It so happened that the little church of San Damiano, where he was praying, was in a state of disrepair. So Francis obeyed our Lord by doing what he could: he started to replace the stones and bricks that had fallen off the church's walls—he started to repair the little church building of San Damiano. That was all the Lord needed, that little gesture of loving and generous obedience was transformed into a religious movement that has pumped new spiritual vitality into the Church and the world ever since. Today, what is the Lord asking you to do, and how will you respond?

• I will review my schedule and commitments and determine where I can make more time to engage in some kind of apostolic activity.

- I will review my budget and see where I can cut down on expenditures in order to give material support to some work of charity and evangelization.

- I will say "yes" to the invitation that I have heard God speaking in my heart for a while, but which I have as yet been to afraid to accept.

- (Write your own resolution) I will_____

Closing Prayer

Blessed are you, Lord God of all creation, for through your goodness we have received the bread we offer you: fruit of the earth and work of human hands, it will become for us the bread of life.

Blessed are you, Lord God of all creation, for through your goodness we have received the wine we offer you: fruit of the vine and work of human hands, it will become our spiritual drink.

With humble spirit and contrite heart may we be accepted by you, O Lord, and may our sacrifice in your sight this day be pleasing to you, Lord God.

—Roman Missal, Offertory Prayers (and private prayer of the priest) at the start of the Liturgy of the Eucharist

Chapter 13
Daily Life Matters

There cannot be two parallel lives in their existence: on the one hand, the so-called "spiritual" life, with its values and demands; and on the other, the so-called "secular" life, that is, life in a family, at work, in social relationships, in the responsibilities of public life and in culture. The branch, engrafted to the vine which is Christ, bears its fruit in every sphere of existence and activity. In fact, every area of the lay faithful's lives, as different as they are, enters into the plan of God, who desires that these very areas be the "places in time" where the love of Christ is revealed and realized for both the glory of the Father and service of others.

—St. John Paul II, *Christifedeles Laici*, 59

JESUS LIVED FOR about thirty-three years here on earth. He spent the first thirty of those years in obscurity. He lived most of that period in a small town off the beaten path, Nazareth. He spent his days learning from his mother, Mary, and his foster father, Joseph, who ran a carpenter shop and probably served as the village handyman. For thirty years the Savior of the world, the Son of God, the incarnate second person of the Blessed Trinity lived the most normal of human lives. No miracles, no extraordinary manifestations of anything, no special privileges, no prodigious signs after the amazing night of his birth. Just normal daily life.

The Value of the Present Moment

Why? Why did Jesus choose this path? Did he spend those thirty years twiddling his thumbs and waiting around for the moment when he would begin to preach and teach and redeem the world? Not at all. Everything Jesus did and said was part of God's divine revelation. It all has a lesson for us. It teaches us about how God sees the world, and about how we are created and called to live our lives. And the thirty years during which Jesus and the Blessed Virgin Mary lived outside the spotlight teaches us that daily life matters.

The relationships, experiences, and activities of daily life construct the primary arena where we love our neighbors as ourselves, where we fulfill our mission. Too often we overlook this. Too often we fantasize about different circumstances that, or so we think, would give us a chance to live life to the full and be all we can be. Too often we think that "mission" necessarily implies going to far-off places. Too often we forget the wise irony contained in the proverbial phrase "the grass is always greener on the other side of the fence."

Living in a state of perpetual regret and self-pity because of the challenges of our daily circumstances—thinking that "real life" is actually waiting somewhere around the corner and off in the future—distracts the soul. In fact, it can blind us to the real graces and opportunities that the Lord never ceases to present to us: "At every time and in every place, God draws close to man. He calls man to seek him, to know him, to love him with all his strength," the *Catechism* reminds us. "He never ceases to call every man to seek him, so as to find life and happiness… God never ceases to draw man to himself" (*CCC*, 1, 30, 27). Jesus didn't wait until he left Nazareth to redeem the world; the redemption of the world, in fact, necessarily passed through those thirty years in Nazareth. And our contribution to that work of redemption necessarily passes through our Nazareth.

Not All Saints Are Supernovas

We see this truth reflected in the lives of the saints. The most well-known saints are those who were called by God to truly extraordinary lives and missions. St. Francis of Assisi received the stigmata and preached miraculously even to wild animals. St. Faustina Kowalska received mystical visions and had mystical conversations with the Lord on a regular basis throughout her entire consecrated life. St. Patrick exercised such spiritual force— in his preaching, leadership, and miracles—that he converted the entire Irish people to Christianity in his own lifetime.... Because of their dramatic character, these extraordinary manifestations of grace capture our attention and can make us think that holiness consists in being like them.

And yet plenty of other saints reached the pinnacle of holiness and fulfilled their mission on earth without ever leaving the confines of their Nazareth. St. Bede entered the monastery as a seven-year-old boy when his parents entrusted his education to the monks. He died there more than sixty years later, having never left the borders of the double monastery in Jarrow, England. St. Thérèse of Lisieux, whose autobiography led to her being named a Doctor of the Church, died at the young age of twenty-four. At the time of her death, the sisters in her convent were at a loss as to what they should put into the death notice that was customary to send to the other convents—that's how normal and unremarkable her brief consecrated life had been, at least from the outside.

St. Gianna Beretta Molla was an Italian wife, mother, and pediatrician. She liked skiing and fashion and lived amid the normal hustle and bustle of family life. Her holiness took root and flourished there, in her Nazareth. And of course St. Joseph himself, patron saint of the Universal Church, lived and died in the dusty obscurity of the literal Nazareth, speaking nary a single word in the Scriptures.

Redemption Is Rooted in Nazareth

The extraordinary manifestations of grace that capture our attention are gifts God gives to the Church in order to boost our faith. But they are not the substance of holiness and happiness. They are not necessary ingredients in the recipe for Christian faithfulness. Rather, they are simply providential works of grace overflowing from daily lives lived in communion with God. To discover and fulfill our mission in life, to love our neighbor as ourselves and thereby build up the kingdom of God, we must not seek first what is extraordinary and dramatic. We must not vainly hanker after spectacular shows of spiritual power. Rather we must strive to be authentic Christians, fully present and engaged in each duty and interaction that meets us in our Nazareth, where redemption is truly rooted. What flows from that, whether dramatic or not, is up to God.

Moses put it well in his last sermon before the Chosen People of Israel crossed into the Promised Land:

> *For this command which I am giving you today is not too wondrous or remote for you. It is not in the heavens, that you should say, "Who will go up to the heavens to get it for us and tell us of it, that we may do it?" Nor is it across the sea, that you should say, "Who will cross the sea to get it for us and tell us of it, that we may do it?" No, it is something very near to you, in your mouth and in your heart, to do it.* (Deuteronomy 30:11–14)

The principles, virtues, and activities explored in these chapters are all related to how we can help love our neighbors by spreading Christ's kingdom. But they can all be applied—indeed, they *must* be applied—first and foremost in our daily lives. God's providence has placed us there. God's love longs to meet us there. God's grace will flow through us there, leading us step-by-step to the fullness of our calling.

Questions for Personal Reflection or Group Discussion

1. What idea in this chapter struck you most and why?

2. Describe the circumstances of your Nazareth: the duties, relationships, and activities that form the warp and woof of your daily life. Where is God inviting you to love more in them?

3. How easy or hard is it for you to believe that God is at work through you in those daily circumstances? Speak to God right now and express your faith that he is present and active in your Nazareth. Ask for the grace to find and follow him there.

4. Hypocrisy is one of the biggest obstacles to building up the kingdom of Christ. When we profess to be Christians, followers of Christ, we are claiming to have certain standards of behavior. When we habitually fail to live up to those standards, or when we habitually make no effort to do so, we create a disconnect between what we say and what we do. When people notice that, it makes them doubt the authenticity of the Christian faith. *If Jesus were real,* they think to themselves, *then his followers would be more coherent.* What will you do today to root out any remnants of hypocrisy in your life?

- I will go to confession as a concrete expression of my sincere desire to let God's grace root out my self-centered tendencies.

- I will pay special attention to one relationship that is challenging for me, asking God to help me see that person as he does, and to help me "love my neighbor as myself" in that particular case.

- I will ask forgiveness from someone I may have offended, consciously or not.

- (Write your own resolution) I will_____

Concluding Prayer

O God, who cause the minds of the faithful
to unite in a single purpose,
grant your people to love what you command
and to desire what you promise,
that, amid the uncertainties of this world,
our hearts may be fixed on that place
where true gladness is found.
May your grace, O Lord, we pray,
at all times go before us and follow after
and make us always determined
to carry out good works.
Through our Lord Jesus Christ, your Son,
who lives and reigns with you in the unity of the Holy Spirit,
one God, for ever and ever. Amen.

—*Roman Missal,* Collects for the Twenty-First and Twenty-Eighth Sundays in Ordinary Time

Chapter 14
Who Is Your Neighbor?

The Lord himself renews his invitation to all the lay faithful to come closer to him every day. And with the recognition that what is his is also their own, they ought to associate themselves with him in his saving mission. Once again he sends them into every town and place where he himself is to come.

—St. John Paul II, *Christifedeles Laici*, 2

JESUS WANTS HIS grace to touch every human heart. He wants to lead every person out of the darkness of sin and frustration and into the spiritual light and fulfillment of his kingdom.

This is good and pleasing to God our savior, who wills everyone to be saved and to come to knowledge of the truth.... He delivered us from the power of darkness and transferred us to the kingdom of his beloved Son, in whom we have redemption, the forgiveness of sins.... For the kingdom of God is not a matter of food and drink, but of righteousness, peace, and joy in the Holy Spirit. (1 Timothy 2:3–4; Colossians 1:13–14; Romans 14:17)

Preparing Hearts for the Lord

Only his grace can work that redemption and pour the Holy Spirit into human hearts. Yet Jesus wants us to be the heralds who announce the Good News of his salvation and so open hearts to receive that grace. This is how he arranged things during his own earthly ministry, and that set the pattern for the rest of human history: "After this the Lord appointed seventy-two others whom he sent ahead of him in pairs to every town and place he intended to visit" (Luke 10:1).

Jesus intends to visit "every town and place" himself. He truly is the Savior, and unless he enters a heart, his kingdom cannot come there. Unless his presence in a heart deepens and expands, his kingdom cannot grow there. But he sends his disciples "ahead of him" to prepare the way, to be messengers of his kingdom and channels of his saving and sanctifying grace. When he commands us to "love your neighbor as yourself," he points out which "town and place" he wants us to go and prepare for him: all the hearts that are within our own actual and potential circles of influence.

Bonum Est Diffusivum Sui

Have you ever noticed that evil is contagious? As the old saying goes, one bad apple spoils the bunch. Sociological studies have explored the influence of "bad apples" in the workplace, finding statistical evidence that even one employee with a habitually sour attitude has a disproportionately negative effect on the entire workplace atmosphere. If you have children, you are keenly aware of the destructive effects that can flow from them hanging out with the wrong kind of peers. Even St. Paul identifies and applies this principle, quoting an ancient proverb: "Do not be led astray: 'Bad company corrupts good morals'" (1 Corinthians 15:33).

But the contrary is also true; goodness is also contagious. An old Latin saying puts it concisely: "Bonum est diffusivum sui" ("Goodness always tends to spread"). If you are a teacher or a coach, you always want students or players who work hard and build up the rest of the class or team. If you are a parent, you want your children to spend time with good kids, knowing this will have a good influence on them.

Jesus's famous images of what a Christian is called to be, which we have already reflected on, invoke this principle. He tells his followers they are "the salt of the earth" and "the light of the world" (Matthew 5:13–14). A little bit of salt flavors a whole plate of food and preserves a much larger cut of meat. One small candle or one small lightbulb can illuminate an entire room and be seen through a window from far away. The goodness and grace that we receive from Christ always tends to spread out and touch those around us—*bonum est diffusivum sui.*

The neighbors we are commanded love, therefore, are first of all every person we come into contact with. Wherever God's providence sends us, whatever lives we touch, we can season them with love, being a blessing to them in small ways or big ways. In this sense, before reflecting on the specific forms of apostolic activity, it is worthwhile to reflect on the circles of influence that every Christian can inject with gospel goodness.

Our Circles of Influence

The circle closest to our own heart is our family, and most especially our immediate family. Then comes the circle of our friends, the people we lean on and the ones who lean on us to make life bearable, enjoyable, and meaningful. The next circle is all of our colleagues and acquaintances, those brought together with us not by our own intention, but through outside circumstances—we go to the same school, we work at the same company, we live in the same neighborhood, we go to the same parish, and so on.

Moving further out, we reach the circle of strangers, those we come into contact with only once and may never meet again, or those we only hear about or know about abstractly—the flight attendant on the plane, the help desk representative we speak to on the phone, the person who reads an article we write, the people affected by a law we help pass, the citizens of a city far away who are suffering from a recent earthquake.

Finally, our circles of influence also include our enemies—those who are actively working against what we are working for, those who are actively obstructing what we are legitimately pursuing.

These circles of influence often overlap, and their borders are porous, so that a stranger can become a friend, for example, or a family member can become an enemy. And any effect we have on any single person in any of those circles of influence will in turn affect that person's interaction with his or her various circles of influence. And as we grow and engage in the activities of life, our circles can also expand and contract.

Beyond Math

Identifying these circles is not meant to turn our lives into some kind of mathematical diagram where we try to categorize and control everyone we meet. Rather, the point is simply to pause and reflect on the truly vast field of influence every human being exerts. Our actions and decisions are like stones being thrown into a quiet lake; their repercussions spread like ripples on the water all the way to the shore.

We don't have to go very far to identify our neighbor. To obey the Lord's command, to find our first and finest field of Christian mission, we only have to seek to treat those within our circles of influence as God would have us, spreading his goodness wherever we go and readying hearts to receive him ever more fully.

Questions for Personal Reflection or Group Discussion

1. What idea in this chapter struck you most and why?

2. Make a drawing that illustrates your different circles of influence. Think about all the people whose lives are touched, directly or indirectly, by your life. How does it make you feel?

3. Which of your circles of influence receives its fair share of your attention? Which one, if any, have you been neglecting, and why?

4. The closer circles of influence deserve our greater attention. Just think, for example, of the busy husband and dad who

spends so much time at work that he neglects his wife and children. He has lost his center, and eventually even the good he is doing in the outer circles will suffer because of it. This is an especially important principle of discernment to keep in mind in our digital age. It's so easy now to stay connected—at least apparently—with hundreds of people. It can lead to a dispersion of attention and a distracting fascination with merely superficial experiences and interactions. Living only on the surface of things, however, impoverishes the soul. What will you do today to keep superficial things in their proper place?

- I will fast from my favorite social media interaction for a day.
- I will refrain from reading the latest headlines for a day.
- I will enjoy a lovely experience, and instead of taking a photo of it, I will simply let it seep into my soul and enrich me.
- (Write your own resolution) I will_____

Concluding Prayer

I leave you now with this prayer: that the Lord Jesus will reveal himself to each one of you, that he will give you the strength to go out and profess that you are Christian, that he will show you that he alone can fill your hearts. Accept his freedom and embrace his truth, and be messengers of the certainty that you have been truly liberated through the death and resurrection of the Lord Jesus. This will be the new experience, the powerful experience, that will generate, through you, a more just society and a better world. God bless you and may the joy of Jesus be always with you!

—St. John Paul II[20]

---

20 Address of His Holiness John Paul II to the Students of the Catholic University; Washington, D.C., October 7, 1979; http://w2.vatican.va/content/john-paul-ii/en/speeches/1979/october/documents/hf_jp-ii_spe_19791007_usa_washington_studenti-univ-catt.html.

Part III
Your Modes of Apostolate

"Therefore do not be afraid of them. Nothing is concealed that will not be revealed, nor secret that will not be known. What I say to you in the darkness, speak in the light; what you hear whispered, proclaim on the housetops. And do not be afraid of those who kill the body but cannot kill the soul; rather, be afraid of the one who can destroy both soul and body in Gehenna. Are not two sparrows sold for a small coin? Yet not one of them falls to the ground without your Father's knowledge. Even all the hairs of your head are counted. So do not be afraid; you are worth more than many sparrows. Everyone who acknowledges me before others I will acknowledge before my heavenly Father. But whoever denies me before others, I will deny before my heavenly Father."

—Matthew 10:26–33

Chapter 15
Your Three Ways to Evangelize

We most earnestly beg all our sons the world over, clergy and laity, to be deeply conscious of the dignity, the nobility, which is theirs through being grafted on to Christ as shoots on a vine: "I am the vine; you the branches." *They are thus called to a share in His own divine life; and since they are united in mind and spirit with the divine Redeemer even when they are engaged in the affairs of the world, their work becomes a continuation of His work, penetrated with redemptive power.* "He that abideth in men, and I in him, the same beareth much fruit."

—St. John XXIII, *Mater et Magistra,* 259

NO ONE WILL evangelize in the exact same way that you do. Your relationship with God is unique, your social network is unique, your circles of influence are unique, and your mission in the Church and the world is unique. And so how you enter into the universal apostolate[21] will also be unique. In a sense there are as many forms of apostolate as there are individual Christians.

---

21 Following the explanations of the first chapters of this book, I am using the terms *evangelization* and *apostolate* interchangeably. To review, here is how the *Catechism* defines *apostolate*: "The whole Church is apostolic, in that she remains, through the successors of St. Peter and the other apostles, in communion of faith and life with her origin: and in that she is 'sent out' into the whole world. All members of the Church share in this mission, though in various ways. The Christian vocation is, of its nature, a vocation to the apostolate as well. Indeed, we call an apostolate, every activity of the Mystical Body that aims to spread the Kingdom of Christ over all the earth" (*CCC*, 863).

In keeping with their vocations [ordained ministers and lay people], the demands of the times and the various gifts of the Holy Spirit, the apostolate assumes the most varied forms. (CCC, 864)

This is why the first requirement for carrying out our apostolic mission is to be good listeners—to listen to the whispers of the Holy Spirit directing our desires, our hopes, our thoughts, our actions.

A Threefold Richness

But the Church has also identified three general categories of apostolate. In fact the Second Vatican Council published an entire decree describing the apostolate of the Church, especially of the laity, called *Apostolicam Actuositatem*. Understanding these general categories will help us be better listeners and more effective apostles.

These three forms of evangelization correspond to the threefold mission of Christ, who redeems and sanctifies the world as priest, prophet-teacher, and king. Through baptism every Christian shares in this threefold mission, though clergy and laity share in different ways.

A Way to Bridge Heaven and Earth

The priestly aspect of our mission consists in bringing God's grace to bear on our normal activities. Everything Jesus did, from working in the carpenter shop to dying on the cross, expressed and exhibited his love for and obedience to the Father. Everything Jesus did was an offering to the Father, an act of worship, part of his redeeming sacrifice that reached its culmination through his passion, death, and resurrection. In this way Jesus reconnected the human realm to the divine realm—a connection that had been lost with original sin. Such is the primary function of a priest—to be a bridge between heaven and earth.

But even the lay members of the Church exercise this function when they unite their daily activities and sacrifices to the offering of Christ himself by living them with faith and by placing them spiritually on the altar during Mass.

> The lay faithful are sharers in the priestly mission, for which Jesus offered himself on the cross and continues to be offered in the celebration of the Eucharist for the glory of God and the salvation of humanity. Incorporated in Jesus Christ, the baptized are united to him and to his sacrifice in the offering they make of themselves and their daily activities…. For their work, prayers and apostolic endeavors, their ordinary married and family life, their daily labor, their mental and physical relaxation, if carried out in the Spirit, and even the hardships of life if patiently borne—all of these become spiritual sacrifices acceptable to God through Jesus Christ. During the celebration of the Eucharist these sacrifices are most lovingly offered to the Father along with the Lord's body. Thus as worshipers whose every deed is holy, the lay faithful consecrate the world itself to God.[22]

In other words, simply the way we live our daily lives—filled with faith, as expressions of love for God and neighbor—can become a powerful witness in the world to the reality and truth of the gospel, as well as an instrument of God's grace.

Words to Change History

The second category of apostolate flows from the prophetic mission of Christ, which also is shared by every Christian. In this context, *prophetic* doesn't simply mean foretelling the future. Rather it refers to "speaking forth" on behalf of God: announcing the gospel, explaining it, and teaching it by words. The clergy do

22 St. John Paul II, *Christifideles Laici,* 14.

this in an official way, but all Christians are called to do so in their efforts to evangelize the world: "To teach in order to lead others to faith is the task of every preacher and of each believer" (*CCC, 904*).

Works to Renew the World

Finally, the third way of evangelizing is linked to Christ's kingly mission, which once again is shared by every Christian. For the clergy, this mission applies particularly to governing the ecclesial structures themselves, although laypersons can also participate in that activity to some extent.[23] Primarily, however, for the laity this form of apostolate has to do with bringing the institutions and conditions of society under the rule of Christ, what the Second Vatican Council called "the renewal of the temporal order":

> *The laity must take up the renewal of the temporal order as their own special obligation…. Moreover, by uniting their forces let the laity so remedy the institutions and conditions of the world when the latter are an inducement to sin, that these may be conformed to the norms of justice, favoring rather than hindering the practice of virtue. By so doing they will impregnate culture and human works with a moral value.[24]*

In short, the three ways of evangelization have to do with our priestly and Christ-centered *way* of day-to-day living, our prophetic *words* of Christian wisdom, and our creative *works* directed toward Christianizing human society, institutions, and culture from the inside out. In the following chapters we will dig into some more specific aspects of each.

---

23 "The laity can also feel called, or be in fact called, to cooperate with their pastors in the service of the ecclesial community, for the sake of its growth and life. This can be done through the exercise of different kinds of ministries according to the grace and charisms which the Lord has been pleased to bestow on them" (*CCC,* 910).

24 The Second Vatican Council, *Apostolicam Actuositatem,* 7; *CCC*, 909.

Questions for Personal Reflection or Group Discussion

1. What idea in this chapter struck you most and why?

2. From the point of view of your sharing in Christ's priestly, prophetic, and kingly mission of redemption, what aspects of your life do *not* have evangelizing potential?

3. How would you describe in your own words the three dimensions of the Church's apostolate?

4. G.K. Chesterton, a famous convert to Catholicism and prolific author and apologist in the early twentieth century, once quipped that when someone becomes a Christian absolutely everything changes, even brushing one's teeth. His point was that once we are members of Christ's mystical body, which happens through baptism, our smallest actions take on grace-filled meaning. What will you do today to activate this meaning more intentionally?

- I will say a small prayer before each of my day's activities, consciously offering them up to God for the advance of his kingdom.

- I will light a devotional candle somewhere in my house, to remind me that, because God inhabits my soul through grace, my house is in a certain sense a Christian sanctuary, an outpost of Christ's kingdom here on earth.

- I will arrive for Mass a few minutes early next time so I can focus my heart and prayerfully place on the altar all my activities, intentions, and relationships, thus uniting them to Christ's self-offering and living more purposefully my share in the Lord's priestly mission.

- (Write your own resolution) I will_____

Concluding Prayer

In the Church, God has made known to us his hidden purpose: to make all things one in Christ. Let us pray that his will may be done.
—Father, unite all things in Christ.

We give you thanks for the presence and power of your Spirit in the Church: give us the will to search for unity, and inspire us to pray and work together.
—Father, unite all things in Christ.

We give you thanks for all whose work proclaims your love: help us to serve the communities in whose life we share.
—Father, unite all things in Christ.

Father, care for all who serve in the Church as ministers of your word and sacraments: may they bring your whole family to the unity for which Christ prayed.
—Father, unite all things in Christ.

Your people have known the ravages of war and hatred: grant that they may know the peace left by your Son.
—Father, unite all things in Christ.

Fulfill the hopes of those who sleep in your peace: bring them to that final resurrection when you will be all in all.
– Father, unite all things in Christ.

—Liturgy of the Hours, Prayers and Intercessions for Evening Prayer for the Sixteenth Sunday in Ordinary Time[25]

---

25 http://www.universalis.com/index.htm.

Chapter 16
Your Moral Witness

Above all the gospel must be proclaimed by witness. Take a Christian or a handful of Christians who, in the midst of their own community, show their capacity for understanding and acceptance, their sharing of life and destiny with other people, their solidarity with the efforts of all for whatever is noble and good. Let us suppose that, in addition, they radiate in an altogether simple and unaffected way their faith in values that go beyond current values, and their hope in something that is not seen and that one would not dare to imagine. Through this wordless witness these Christians stir up irresistible questions in the hearts of those who see how they live: Why are they like this? Why do they live in this way? What or who is it that inspires them? Why are they in our midst? Such a witness is already a silent proclamation of the Good News and a very powerful and effective one. Here we have an initial act of evangelization.

—Blessed Paul VI, *Evangelii Nuntiandi*, 21

GOD DIDN'T SAVE us from a distance. In Jesus he became one of us, walked along the paths of life with real human beings through the streets of Palestine, and made his redeeming love and grace tangible. And he did that for thirty years before he preached his first sermon. Since every Christian is *alter Christus* (another Christ), every Christian should do the same.

Christian Billboards

This is one of the meanings of "witness" or "testimony." Our outward behavior shows forth the truth, the goodness, and the beauty of Jesus Christ. We become, as it were, billboards and advertisements for the abundant life Jesus gives when people accept his kingship and become his followers.

Of course, first of all, moral integrity is its own reward. Living in accord with what is morally right means living in accord with what will lead us toward the fulfillment we long for; it's following the manufacturer's instructions—the manufacturer of human nature being God and the moral law being the instructions for how to make human nature flourish. Telling the truth, honoring our elders, obeying legitimate authority, promoting human life, respecting other people's property, treating people with the dignity they deserve as children of God, courageously facing up to evil and corruption, wisely training and governing our raw emotions and passions, putting our gifts and talents at the service of others— these are clearly steps on the road to spiritual maturity and lasting happiness for anyone who takes them.

And yet they have a corollary effect as well. The more faithful we are to the moral law God has built into the universe, the sharper images of God himself we become. We were created in his image and likeness, but that original identity was obscured by sin and evil. As God's grace works in our lives, and as we cooperate with that grace through freely engaging in the battle for moral integrity and spiritual maturity, that original identity is gradually restored and even enhanced. Our personal existence begins to resonate with God's glory. We become mirrors of God's love and wisdom. We begin to "shine like lights in the world"—a world that is darkened with greed and lust and superficial folly (see Philippians 2:15). We become, without even thinking about it, a scent of heaven that captures the attention of other people and makes them curious: "For we are the aroma of Christ for God among those who are being saved and among those who are perishing" (2 Corinthians 2:15).

Our own moral and spiritual growth brings us interior peace and strength and overflows into the world around us; God uses it to invite others to step onto the same path of redemption we are following. This is the first and indispensable form of apostolate for every Christian.

When the Laws Were Not Friendly

In the first centuries of Christianity, this was in many ways the *only* form of apostolate. Christianity was outlawed. Public displays of faith and public evangelizing activities, therefore, were minimal at best and life-threatening at worst. And yet the Church continued to attract new members. It continued to grow and expand at a truly remarkable rate. How?

Because of the moral witness of the Christians: While still living within the Roman Empire, their faith liberated them from Rome's pagan prejudices and vices. And as a result the moral and spiritual quality of their lives increased drastically. People saw how the Christians lived, it resonated in their hearts, and they wanted to find for themselves that same purpose, depth, and joy. Thus Christianity spread through the silent, moral witness of healthy Christian living.

The Beauty and Power of Martyrdom

Sometimes this witness extended beyond the calm interactions of daily life and became dramatic. The English word *martyr*, in fact, comes from the Greek word for "witness." The early Christian martyrs gave definitive and irresistible witness to the truth of the gospel. These Christians modeled moral integrity through their example of honesty, responsibility, and charity; they modeled spiritual maturity through their courageous fidelity to the unseen realities revealed by Christ, like the Real Presence in the Eucharist and the promise of heaven and eternal life. In addition their example and fidelity endured the hardest test of all: physical and emotional torture—and even death.

St. Lawrence the Deacon was one of these early martyrs, or witnesses, to Christ. He resisted the Roman government's efforts to unjustly intrude on the interior life of the Church. For doing so he was condemned to execution by burning—a truly horrible fate. The night before his martyrdom was spent in a dank prison cell, but instead of bemoaning his fate, he dedicated the whole night to prayer and song, joyfully preparing to meet the Lord. Unbeknownst to St. Lawrence, his pagan guard, Romanus, was watching closely, and such strange behavior caught his attention. The soldier's curiosity led him to question the saint, who gladly explained the Christian faith behind his calm confidence in the face of such humiliation and suffering. Soon Lawrence was baptizing Romanus right there in the prison cell.

Our moral and spiritual witness is our first apostolate. Simply through engaging in the struggle to develop the moral integrity and spiritual maturity we are called to allows God's grace to fill our souls and shine forth in surprising ways, catching the attention of our neighbors and opening their hearts to hear news of the kingdom. It is a primary way to love your neighbor as yourself.

Questions for Personal Reflection or Group Discussion

1. What idea in this chapter struck you most and why?

2. When have you been positively influenced by someone's moral and spiritual witness? Remember, savor, and thank God for that experience.

3. In which circumstances in your life do you find it hardest to maintain your moral witness to Christ? Why do you think those situations/relationships tend to be so challenging, and what are you going to do about it?

4. Many Christians complain that the moral standards of today's culture are so upside down that it makes it impossible to live with the integrity we are called to live. And yet that point of view fails to take into account at least two important factors. First, God himself is at work in our souls through his grace. If we cultivate that grace through prayer, study, and the sacraments, it will give us all the strength we need to do what is right. Second, throughout history the Church has frequently had to face aggressively corrosive socio-cultural environments. In fact Jesus himself predicted this: *"In the world you will have trouble,"* he promised his disciples during the Last Supper (John 16:33). And yet, the Church has often ended up influencing the culture itself more than allowing the culture to corrupt the Church. What will you do today to strengthen your moral witness in a world gone morally mad?

- I will do a hidden act of kindness without seeking any reward.

- I will make sure to speak truthfully in every conversation and meeting I have today, refraining from exaggerations and deceptions that only feed my vanity.

- I will do something special for someone close to me—spouse, parent, sibling—just to show them I love them.

- (Write your own resolution) I will_____

Concluding Prayer

It is truly right and just, our duty and our salvation,
always and everywhere to give you thanks,
Lord, holy Father, almighty and eternal God.
For you are glorified when your saints are praised;
their very sufferings are but wonders of your might:
in your mercy you give ardor to their faith,
to their endurance you grant firm resolve,

and in their struggle the victory is yours,
through Christ our Lord.
Be merciful now to me, and grant me the grace I need be true to
your will in my life today, that my witness may shine like a light
in this darkened world and spread the sweet aroma of Christ to
those around me who need it. Amen.

—Adapted from Preface II of Holy Martyrs in the *Roman Missal*

Chapter 17
The Apostolate of Kindness

*Without repeating everything that we have already mentioned,
it is appropriate first of all to emphasize the following point: for
the Church, the first means of evangelization is the witness of an
authentically Christian life, given over to God in a communion that
nothing should destroy and at the same time given to one's neighbor
with limitless zeal. As we said recently to a group of lay people,
"Modern man listens more willingly to witnesses than to teachers,
and if he does listen to teachers, it is because they are witnesses."*

—Blessed Paul VI, *Evangelii Nuntiandi*, 41

AT ONE POINT, the Bible sums up Jesus's life on earth with the simple phrase, "He went about doing good…" (Acts 10:38). When it comes to the witness of our lives in this world, to becoming a mirror of God's love for those around us, a better program is hard to formulate. Doing unto others what we would have them do to us, loving our neighbors as ourselves, involves at the very least the habitual disposition to do good and not harm to those around us.

Distasteful Do-Gooders

In some circles the term "do-gooder" has taken on derogatory connotations. Maybe that's because so many do-gooders are, in some way or another, hypocritical. They go about doing good, but with ulterior motives. They are expecting something in return—praise, popularity, payback. Their appearance of being concerned for others masks a self-centered approach to life. And so, when whomever they want to impress or influence isn't around, their mask falls away and they revert to pettiness and even cruelty in attitude, speech, and action. If you want to know a person's true colors, so they say, watch how he or she behaves when nobody is looking.

That kind of hypocritical behavior clouds our soul. It inhibits our own spiritual growth as well as obscuring our capacity to mirror God's goodness. But it doesn't negate the importance of living with an eye for kindness, of following the example of our Lord who "went about doing good." Kindness, the quality of being friendly, generous, and considerate, is certainly not the pinnacle of moral integrity or the sum total of holiness. But unkindness, being inconsiderate and harsh, is just as certainly incompatible with both. To be kind to others, especially those in need, is the entrance level in the edifice of love.

Why Kindness Matters

From a theological perspective, kindness flows from the recognition that every person we meet was created in God's image and likeness, redeemed by Christ's atoning sacrifice on the cross, and called to everlasting life in communion with the Lord and all the saints of heaven. That's every human being, every person we see, hear about, run into, interact with—every single one. As Pope Benedict XVI put it in his inaugural homily as pope: "We are not some casual and meaningless product of evolution. Each of us is the result of a thought of God. Each of us is willed, each of us is loved, each of us is necessary."[26]

---

26 Benedict XVI, homily, April, 24, 2005; http://w2.vatican.va/content/benedict-xvi/en/homilies/2005/documents/hf_ben-xvi_hom_20050424_inizio-pontificato.html.

This may seem obvious to those of us who have grown up in the Church, but it isn't obvious to citizens of this fallen world. It's something that was revealed to us by Jesus. Before the Christian era and beyond the influence of Christian culture, universal human dignity was and is only vaguely perceived—at best. In non-Christian cultures kindness was and is reserved for people of your own group or caste. Outsiders are automatically considered enemies and threats, not brothers and sisters, until proven otherwise. This logic has produced a large portion of the horrendous injustices that litter the path of human history.

This is not to say that all Christians perfectly follow our Lord's example—non-Christians don't have a monopoly on sin. But the truth that, by nature, every human being deserves to be loved as we love ourselves is a truth that Jesus needed to reveal. Our sin-darkened minds needed the divine light to perceive it clearly.

Words from the Word

Jesus illustrated the importance of this kindness—authentic kindness, not conditional and hypocritical kindness—multiple times. In the Sermon on the Mount, for example, he pointed out that our disposition to do good for others should be habitual and universal, just as God's is:

"You have heard that it was said, 'You shall love your neighbor and hate your enemy.' But I say to you, love your enemies, and pray for those who persecute you, that you may be children of your heavenly Father, for he makes his sun rise on the bad and the good, and causes rain to fall on the just and the unjust. For if you love those who love you, what recompense will you have? Do not the tax collectors do the same? And if you greet your brothers only, what is unusual about that? Do not the pagans do the same? So be perfect, just as your heavenly Father is perfect." (Matthew 5:43–48)

In the same passage, Jesus talked about carrying someone's burden an extra mile when you only really *have* to carry it (by law) for one mile. He talked about handing over both your tunic and your cloak when someone demands only your cloak. He talked about turning the other cheek in response to humiliations—what St. Paul later described in less metaphorical terms:

> *Let love be sincere; hate what is evil, hold on to what is good; love one another with mutual affection; anticipate one another in showing honor.... Bless those who persecute [you], bless and do not curse them.... If possible, on your part, live at peace with all.... Do not be conquered by evil but conquer evil with good. (Romans 12:9–10, 14, 18, 21)*

This is how a Christian is supposed to behave in the world, and this is a fundamental element in how we bear witness to the truth of God's revelation in Christ:

> *"I give you a new commandment: love one another. As I have loved you, so you also should love one another. This is how all will know that you are my disciples, if you have love for one another." (John 13:34–35)*

Kindness versus Weakness

Kindness is not weakness. Kindness doesn't require that we turn ourselves into doormats or become enablers of other people's dysfunctions. Kindness is "going about doing good," and what is truly good for another person will never involve condoning their sin or bolstering their unhealthy coping mechanisms. That would be falling into the trap of crippling codependency. Kindness means staying aware of the needs of our fellow pilgrims as we all make our way along life's journey—and helping them out whenever we can. It's that simple.

St. Thomas More, a layman who was chancellor of England and friend and confidante to King Henry VIII in the sixteenth century, showed a memorable act of kindness just moments before he was martyred. He had refused to accept Henry's repudiation of the Catholic faith, a repudiation that the king promulgated as a law for the entire country when he established the independent Church of England. As a result, St. Thomas was imprisoned and eventually beheaded. When he stepped onto the scaffold, the executioner—as was customary—asked for the victim's forgiveness before performing his deed. St. Thomas embraced him warmly and, sensing the man's anxiety, reassured him, saying with a smile, "Pick up thy Spirits, Man, and be not afraid to do thine Office. My Neck is very short, take heed therefore thou strike not awry…"[27] It was a word of kindness—even a cheerful jest—spoken in a moment when kind gestures would be least expected: a fitting conclusion for a life whose daily witness to God's goodness was capped with the martyr's crown.

Perhaps St. Thomas More's kindness on the executioner's block flowed from the faith-filled knowledge that he was only moments away from his definitive encounter with the Lord. Indeed, St. Paul linked his exhortation on Christian kindness to an awareness of Christ's closeness, implying that only through faith and grace can we answer our call to the apostolate of kindness by "going about doing good": "Your kindness should be known to all," he wrote to the Christians in Philippi, adding: "The Lord is near" (Philippians 4:5).

Questions for Personal Reflection or Group Discussion

1. What idea in this chapter struck you most and why?

2. How would you describe in your own words the difference between hypocritical or conditional kindness and authentic Christian kindness? When you find it hard to be kind, does that necessarily mean your kindness is hypocritical? Why or why not?

---

27 *The Trial of Sir Thomas More;* http://law2.umkc.edu/faculty/projects/ftrials/more/moretrialreport.html.

3. Acts of kindness will flow naturally from an attitude of true respect and esteem for others. In which of your circles of influence do you find it harder to maintain such an attitude and why?

4. Sometimes we can fall into the error of thinking that our missionary activity as Christians has to take place far from home. But the truth is that we don't need to go to a country far away or a neighborhood on the other side of the city in order to engage in the apostolate of kindness—a true form of evangelization, as the quotation from Blessed Pope Paul VI at the beginning of this chapter makes clear. At times a distant mission trip will help spark or rejuvenate our faith, as can a pilgrimage to an important Christian shrine—these experiences take us out of our routines and can create some space for a fresh encounter with God. And certainly there are many parts of the world where people are suffering horribly and in dire need of aid. But in order to mature spiritually, we must also give due importance to the apostolate of kindness in all our circles of influence, perhaps most especially in the first one, the one closest to home, that of our own families. Living consistent and sincere kindness in the home is hard—it's much easier to be kind to people we don't have to live with. What will you do today to engage in the apostolate of kindness?

• I will express honest interest in knowing how my immediate family members are feeling about what's going on in their lives.

• I will volunteer to help out with something I normally try to avoid.

• I will interrupt my own activities when I detect that someone around me needs a kind word or a bit of help.

• (Write your own resolution) I will_____

Concluding Prayer

Lord, make me an instrument of your peace.
Where there is hatred, let me sow love;
where there is injury, pardon;
where there is doubt, faith;
where there is despair, hope;
where there is darkness, light;
where there is sadness, joy.

O, Divine Master, grant that I may not so much seek to be
consoled as to console;
to be understood as to understand;
to be loved as to love;
For it is in giving that we receive;
it is in pardoning that we are pardoned;
it is in dying that we are born again to eternal life.[28]

—Prayer of St. Francis of Assisi

---

28 http://www.catholic.org/prayers/prayer.php?p=134.

Chapter 18
But What If I Don't Feel Like It?

[T]he Christian vocation is also directed toward the apostolate, toward evangelization, toward mission. All baptized persons are called by Christ to become his apostles in their own personal situation and in the world: "As the Father has sent me, so I send you" *(John 20:21). Through his Church Christ entrusts you with the fundamental mission of sharing with others the gift of salvation, and he invites you to participate in building his kingdom. He chooses you, in spite of the personal limitations everyone has, because he loves you and believes in you. This unconditional love of Christ should be the very soul of your apostolic work, in accord with the words of St Paul:* "The love of Christ impels us" *(2 Corinthians 5:14). Being disciples of Christ is not a private matter. On the contrary, the gift of faith must be shared with others.*

—St. John Paul II[29]

SOMETIMES KINDNESS OVERFLOWS effortlessly from a warm and affectionate heart. At other times that same heart feels cold and antagonistic, and even the possibility of kindness is crowded back into a hidden corner of the soul. What's going on when we feel that way? What are we supposed to do about it? We have to

---

29 St. John Paul II, Message for the VII World Youth Day, November 24, 1991; http://w2.vatican.va/content/john-paul-ii/en/messages/youth/documents/ hf_jp-ii_mes_24111991_vii-world-youth-day.html.

wrestle a little bit with this question, and we will do so by looking at attitudes and actions.

Disobedient Feelings

Regarding attitudes, we cannot underestimate the importance of distinguishing between unwilled feelings—spontaneous emotional reactions—and willed decisions. Because of our fallen human nature, our feelings are not always obedient to our faith. We can feel an emotional repugnance toward prayer, for example, even though we firmly believe in the importance and value of prayer. Just so, we can feel an emotional disconnect or distaste toward another person, even though we firmly believe that person is created in God's image, loved by God unconditionally, redeemed by Christ's sacrifice on the cross, called to eternal communion with God in heaven, and therefore deserving of our kindness.

Subjective Emotions

Those spontaneous, negative feelings can trace their origin to passing subjective factors, such as tiredness or a bad mood induced by the weather or hormonal fluctuations. They can also stem from subconscious factors—an intangible quality of the other person, for example, may trigger in us a reaction linked to hidden emotional patterns that were formed before we were even self-conscious. These same subconscious factors can be at play in our natural affections and likes: We feel more or less affinity toward Person A simply because his personality somehow harmonizes well with the emotional needs that have been more or less seared into the substrata of our own personality. In these cases feelings of repugnance toward someone are completely unwilled. They are not sinful.

And yet they can be valuable for our own growth in self-knowledge. They are giving us information, and we may grow significantly in self-knowledge through reflecting on their origins and what they reveal about our own interior life. Sometimes they are linked to deep wounds that may need some psychological treatment. Often they simply are linked to normal wounds that can become fruitful catalysts for spiritual growth when we identify them and integrate them into our prayer life.

Objective Emotions

On the other hand, negative emotions toward other people can also be caused by objective factors. If another person habitually makes self-centered decisions and so becomes a burden for those around them, this will become a source of tension and perhaps even anger. We see Jesus, for instance, becoming angry with the Pharisees when they simply refused to listen to him, consistently closing their hearts and minds to his saving message.

These emotional reactions are objectively linked to damaging actions of other people, and they also are valuable as sources of information. They are telling us something about the relationship—something is wrong, something is unjust, something needs to be dealt with or changed in order to reorient the relationship and make it healthy. These emotional reactions are not willfully chosen; they happen almost automatically, so they, too, cannot be sinful. They just *are*.

Sometimes objective emotional reactions can be exacerbated by subjective factors, forming a potent emotional cocktail that often produces exaggerated reactions.

The Right Attitude

And so, clearly the right attitude toward these emotional experiences has to start with humble acceptance. The emotions are there. They are linked to who you are. They are giving you information. They are not evil in themselves, and so they are nothing to be ashamed of or frustrated about. Accept them. Understand them. But don't put them in the driver's seat of your soul.

Our moral responsibility always inhabits the realm of our free actions, so we are not morally responsible for these unwilled emotional reactions. Our responsibility surfaces with regard to how we decide to deal with the emotions that spontaneously surge up in our souls. The bottom line here is that we should not make our choices based solely on emotion, which would be the epitome of immaturity. Rather, we need to make our decisions based on truth—moral truth and the truths of our faith.

Thus, for example, when I feel an emotional distaste toward prayer, I don't stop praying. Instead I humbly persevere regardless of the negative feelings, even though I may reflect on why I am feeling that repugnance and try to learn from it.

Acting "As If..."

In the case of repugnance toward others, which threatens to manifest itself in unkindness, the same principle applies. I should treat them, to the extent that is possible for me, *as if* I felt the love I know they deserve as God's child. This is virtuous action, a free choice to love, in spite of contrary feelings. And that love means that I treat them with respect and kindness, willing what is good for them. My actions toward them, then, are consistent with my faith and the commandments of the Lord. I don't torture them, abuse them, talk badly about them behind their back, insult and humiliate them, and so on. I try to help them, affirm them, and encourage them.

Sometimes our subjective repugnance toward someone may be so strong—again, not because we will it, which would be sinful, but just because that's the way it is—that we actually need to avoid that person in order not to treat him or her poorly. This can be painful for us—we wish we didn't have such strong negative emotions toward this person. It hurts our pride to experience our brokenness and woundedness so palpably. But the right action is to avoid, as much as it is possible, situations where we know that our emotions have a chance to get the better of us. Pray for that person. Don't harm that person. Be civil and kind to that person when you have to interact with him or her. But until God's grace heals you a little bit more, until you develop more virtue, you may need to minimize your contact with that person.

Actions as Reactions

In the second case—the case of the objective negative emotions that flow from identifiably problematic behaviors and behavior patterns—the kind and loving thing to do is to communicate about it. Talk with the other person about the behavior patterns, try to understand what's behind them, and try to calmly express why they are so bothersome or destructive. Try to help each other adjust the patterns. This is especially the case if your relationship with the person in question is habitual—if you have to continue to interact with him or her on a regular basis.

In some cases you may run into a person who is not willing to change. He or she won't acknowledge destructive behaviors or take responsibility for them. In that circumstance you may need to sever the relationship, at least temporarily. It is not an expression of love to continue enabling someone's dysfunctional behavior by exhibiting the kind of toleration that tacitly approves of it.

In summary, our spontaneous emotional reactions give us information, and until we are mature enough in Christ that those emotions are in perfect sync with the truths of our faith, they will sometimes clash with those truths. That's OK. Accept that and seek to understand it. But don't let it drive your actions and decisions. Pray for grace and strength to always act in accordance with your faith, with God's will, even if your feelings disagree. Live the apostolate of kindness even when it's tough. Gradually, with God's help, your feelings will catch up to your faith and line up more fully with God's will, increasing the energy at your disposal for loving God and loving your neighbor.

Questions for Personal Reflection or Group Discussion

1. What idea in this chapter struck you most and why?
2. How often do you tend to let your feelings alone drive your decisions and actions? In what specific circumstances does this happen most frequently, and why?
3. How do you feel when you sincerely pray for people even though you do not feel a natural affection for them?
4. We can fall into two extremes when it comes to our emotional experiences. We can repress our emotions, because so often they seem to pull us in a different direction from where our faith is leading us. Or we can abandon ourselves to our emotions, becoming their slaves, refusing to do anything we don't feel like doing moment by moment. Christian maturity follows a path between these two extremes. We recognize that emotional experience is a gift from God, but we also recognize that our feelings need to be educated and integrated into the deeper levels of faith and freedom. What will you do today to pursue that integration and emotional maturity?

- If I tend toward the extreme of repression, I will take some time to write in a journal about the emotions I most frequently experience, trying to name, claim, tame, and aim them.

- If I tend toward the extreme of emotionalism, I will take some time to come up with a strategy regarding how to respond proactively to situations where I know I tend to give too much rein to my feelings.

- I will think about a person in my life whom I feel an emotional repugnance toward, and I will try to understand, accept, and maturely deal with those feelings.

- (Write your own resolution) I will_____

Concluding Prayer

With all my heart I seek You; let me not stray from Your commands…. Open my eyes, that I may consider the wonders of Your law. I am a wayfarer of earth; hide not Your commands from me…. Make me understand the way of Your precepts, and I will meditate on Your wondrous deeds…. Your compassion is great, O Lord…. To you, Almighty Father, Creator of the universe and of mankind, through Christ, the Living One, Lord of time and history, in the Spirit who makes all things holy, be praise and honor and glory now and for ever. Amen!

—Psalm 119:10, 18–19, 27, 156; Prayer for the Great Jubilee by St. John Paul II

Chapter 19
Talking Like a Christian

The invitation I offer you to responsibility, to engagement, is first of all an invitation to search for "the truth that will make you free" (John 8:32), and the truth is Christ (cf. John 14:6). And so it is an invitation to place the truth of Christ at the center of your life to give witness to this truth in the story of your daily life, in the decisive choices you have to make, in order to help humanity set its feet firmly on the path of peace and of justice.

—St. John Paul II[30]

ST. PHILIP NERI, the tireless apostle of Renaissance Rome, had a gift for helping people understand Christian teaching. One time he explained the repercussions of careless and uncharitable speech by giving an unusual penance to someone who admitted to those sins in his confession. St. Philip advised the penitent to fill a pillowcase with goose feathers, walk up to the top of a tall hill outside the city walls, and throw all the feathers into the wind. Then, admonished the saint, try to gather up all the feathers that were blown hither and thither.

An impossible task, surely. But a vivid illustration of the power of words—once we have spoken them (or tweeted them,

30 St. John Paul II, Message for XIX World Communications Day, April, 15 1985; http://www.catholicradioassociation.org/World%20Communications%20 Day%20Messages.pdf.

or messaged them, or Facebooked them, or YouTubed them), we cannot retract them. Hence the importance of learning to talk like a Christian—to use words as Christ would have us, thus witnessing on *behalf* of his kingdom and not *against* it.

Seasoned with Salt

So much good can be done with our words! Words can warm cold hearts, enlighten confused minds, and motivate discouraged souls. Words can establish and bolster trust, confidence, community, and human solidarity. The more we understand and master virtue and skill in this arena, the more good we can do—for ourselves and for others—with everything we say.

St. Paul expresses this multiple times in his New Testament writings. He almost always refers to virtuous speech—speech that builds up the community and spreads truth and goodness—in his lists of essentially Christian behaviors, behaviors that image Christ to the world. In his Letter to the Colossians, for example, he writes: "Let your speech always be gracious, seasoned with salt, so that you know how you should respond to each one" (Colossians 4:6). His Letter to the Ephesians goes into more detail:

> *Therefore, putting away falsehood, speak the truth, each one to his neighbor, for we are members one of another.... No foul language should come out of your mouths, but only such as is good for needed edification, that it may impart grace to those who hear. (Ephesians 4:25, 29)*

Words really do matter. Our words can "impart grace," according to St. Paul, becoming vehicles of salvation. But they can just as easily be vehicles of destruction: "Death and life are in the power of the tongue" (Proverbs 18:21).

The Tongue Is a Fire

In his New Testament letter, St. James picks up on this same theme.

He not only shows the apparently disproportionate impact of such a small organ as the tongue, but he also explicitly links virtue in speech with spiritual maturity. He writes:

> *If anyone does not fall short in speech, he is a perfect man, able to bridle his whole body also. If we put bits into the mouths of horses to make them obey us, we also guide their whole bodies. It is the same with ships: even though they are so large and driven by fierce winds, they are steered by a very small rudder wherever the pilot's inclination wishes. In the same way the tongue is a small member and yet has great pretensions. Consider how small a fire can set a huge forest ablaze. The tongue is also a fire. It exists among our members as a world of malice, defiling the whole body and setting the entire course of our lives on fire, itself set on fire by Gehenna. (James 3:1–6)*

Evil or foolish words cause damage—sometimes horrible damage. These biblical passages make that clear. Yet the Bible's descriptions tell us only what we have all experienced: the blow that comes from being slandered or wickedly criticized takes a long time—sometimes a lifetime—to lose its sting.

Evil words only work such great mischief, however, because the power of words has such great potential for good. "The corruption of the best is the worst," as Aristotle put it. Yes, evil men "sharpen their tongues like swords" (Psalm 64:3), but a sharp sword can be useful for good as well as for evil. A sharp knife is necessary for proper surgery and good cooking; a sharp axe is more effective at chopping wood than a dull one. Words can be used to sin, but as St. James points out, "This need not be so" (James 3:10).

Words without Truth

To use words for good, we need first and foremost to avoid the sinful abuse of words. The most common temptations in this area include violations of the truth through lying, rash judgment, calumny, flattery, and adulation. A lie is an intentional deception of someone who has a reasonable claim on the truth. Rash judgment claims to know the interior motive of someone's action and jumps to a judgmental (and, more often than not, false) conclusion about it, whether that conclusion is voiced only interiorly or also out loud. Calumny is deliberately spreading false or exaggerated affirmations about another person to the detriment of his or her good honor, which always has truly noxious repercussions. Flattery and adulation have to do with exaggerated praise, whether motivated by a desire to manipulate (flattery) or an overblown, unreasonable, and blinding sense of reverence (adulation).

Other temptations to abuse the power of language adhere to the truth, but they use it as a weapon of unjust attack instead of an instrument promoting justice and charity. These include detraction, destructive criticism, disparaging irony, and boasting.

Words that Wound

Detraction is often confused with calumny, but it involves an important distinction. Detraction holds to the truth. Detraction is not lying. Yet it yields some of the same hideous by-products of calumny. According to the *Catechism*, someone falls into the temptation of detraction "who, without objectively valid reason, discloses another's faults and failings to persons who did not know them" (*CCC*, 2477). Calumny invents untrue faults and failings about people and spreads them around. Detraction takes people's true faults and failings and turns them into casual conversation topics, often leading to tale-bearing and toxic gossip.

Like detraction, degrading irony and destructive criticism adhere to the truth, but they still qualify as abusive uses of communication. Unlike detraction, however, these forms of speech address directly the person being cut down. Insults like these sometimes burst out during angry arguments, like verbal blows meant to punish, humiliate, or intimidate someone we feel has wronged us. At other times we wield them with calculated purpose in order to manipulate others and get what we want. In certain contexts and relationships, these forms of verbal abuse become barely perceptible habits, ingrained patterns of behavior that need to be rooted out through repentance and the renewing power of grace.

Good-humored irony brings enjoyment, laughter, and stimulation to conversation. When irony wounds other people, however, it crosses the line from spice to poison. Sincere concern for others requires us to pay attention to the effect our comments have on those around us. What one person may take in stride and enjoy may feel like a slap in the face or a personal attack to someone else. When laughter is bought at the expense of someone's tears, the price is simply too high.

The *Catechism* warns against boasting or bragging in the same paragraph where it warns against degrading irony. A boast may include a dose of the truth, but more often than not it also includes an exaggeration. Even more than faulting against the truth, however, boasting mimics degrading irony in its attempt to belittle other people. When I brag, I am attempting to elevate myself over others—the tone and often the content of a boast show a certain disdain for people who have achieved less than I have. Instead of drawing people together and encouraging them, this kind of speech demeans and discourages.

The Talking Apostle

These corrosive forms of communication often have roots in our own insecurities and fears. As Jesus said, "From the fullness of the heart the mouth speaks" (Luke 6:45). Sometimes they erupt from undisciplined passions. Whatever their cause and wherever they appear—in conversation, print, or digital platforms—they counteract the true purpose of speech, which is to communicate truth and build interpersonal communion.

As our spiritual lives mature, these negative behavior patterns gradually fall away and give room to a manner of communicating that better witnesses to the Lord's desire to redeem and save every person—words that express what we really feel and think in ways that also enlighten, encourage, and edify, even when they have to communicate truths that are hard to hear. In that way talking like a Christian becomes an ongoing answer to the call of evangelization.

Questions for Personal Reflection or Group Discussion

1. What idea in this chapter struck you most and why?

2. Which of the temptations mentioned in this chapter do you struggle with most often (lying, calumny, flattery, adulation, detraction, boasting, harsh irony, destructive criticism)? Why? How can you begin to intentionally improve in that area?

3. How would you describe the difference between *destructive* and *constructive* criticism? How is that distinction relevant in your life?

4. Often *what* we say is almost less important than *how* we say it. To really connect with other people requires learning to listen, so that our conversations become meaningful exchanges and not just alternating monologues. We can all improve our listening skills if we put in a little effort. What will you do today to become a better listener so you can also talk more like a Christian?

    •   I will make some space for silence in my day, giving myself a chance to slow down and drink in the sights and sounds of God's creation or of some well-loved works of art, or just to sit and think a bit.

    •   During a conversation or meeting, I will try to repeat back to the person I am conversing with what I think he or she means before launching into what I think about it.

• I will ask someone what he or she thinks or feels about something before trying to express how I think or feel about it.

• (Write your own resolution) I will_____

Concluding Prayer

Set out anew from Christ, you who have found mercy.
Set out anew from Christ, you who have forgiven and been forgiven.
Set out anew from Christ, you who have known pain and suffering.
Set out anew from Christ, you who are tempted by tepidity: the year of grace is endless.
Set out anew from Christ, Church of the new millennium.
Sing as you go!
May Mary, Mother of the Church, Star of Evangelization, accompany us on our journey, as she remained with the disciples on the day of Pentecost. To her we turn with confidence. Through her intercession may the Lord grant us the gift of perseverance in our missionary duty, which is a matter for the entire Church community.

—St. John Paul II, Message for
World Mission Sunday 2001[31]

31 St. John Paul II, Message for World Mission Sunday 2001, June 3, 2001; http://w2.vatican.va/content/john-paul-ii/en/messages/missions/documents/hf_jp-ii_mes_20010607_world-day-for-missions-2001.html.

Chapter 20
Your Pursuit of Excellence

Every activity, every situation, every precise responsibility—as, for example, skill and solidarity in work, love and dedication in the family and the education of children, service to society and public life and the promotion of truth in the area of culture— are the occasions ordained by Providence for a continuous exercise of faith, hope and charity. The Second Vatican Council has invited all the lay faithful to this unity of life by forcefully decrying the grave consequences in separating faith from life, and the gospel from culture: "The Council exhorts Christians, as citizens of one city and the other, to strive to perform their earthly duties faithfully in response to the spirit of the gospel...."

—St. John Paul II, *Christifedeles Laici,* 59

SEEKING EXCELLENCE IN the normal activities and responsibilities of life is part of our Christian witness. When we give our best to do our best in all our works, we are imaging God's love and concern for his own "work" of creation: "In the beginning, God created the heavens and the earth.... God looked at everything he had made, and found it very good" (Genesis 1:1, 31). We are also showing our gratitude toward God for giving us the grace to join our own efforts to his as we "cultivate and care for" the world that has been "given to the children of Adam" (Genesis 2:15; Psalm 115:16).

Whether it's baking cookies, building a house, drafting a law, or entering data into a spreadsheet, human work always shares in human dignity, precisely because it is human, and as such it, too, can be part of the apostolate of witness, part of our way of living the gospel. St. Paul expressed this with his usual brevity and vividness: "So whether you eat or drink, or whatever you do, do everything for the glory of God" (1 Corinthians 10:31).

The Monks Got It Right (at Least in Theory)

The monastic movement that emerged in the early Middle Ages included this often-overlooked dimension of human life in the motto that summed up its core values: *ora et labora* ("pray and work"). Monastic communities sought to worship God directly through prayer (especially community, liturgical prayer) and indirectly through excellence in work. Monasteries became real schools that taught and cultivated the art of living in a period when the civilized world was descending into social and political chaos. Monks followed (and still follow) a disciplined daily schedule, combining work, prayer, and study in a balanced rhythm that allowed for the calm pursuit of excellence in each of those arenas. The results were spectacular. Not only did the monasteries become engines of holiness, they also became motors of human advancement, oases of culture that preserved and became the seeds of a new, Christian civilization.

Even today when you visit one of the ancient monasteries, you feel a certain peace and reverence almost emanating from the walls themselves. The physical elements of the monastery, fruit of the monks' labor over the centuries, have taken on an air of beauty and meaning that turns them into songs of praise preserved in stone. The faithfully pursued ideal of *ora et labora,* working hard and praying hard, created a unity of life that resonates with God's original plan for the human person.

Elevated from Within

The monks lived this unity of life in the cloister, infusing their mundane work with spiritual meaning and thereby pursuing excellence in even the smallest labors. All Christians, however, are called to seek the same ideal in the context of their particular circumstances. St. John Paul II expressed this beautifully in an encyclical letter dedicated entirely to the theme of human work:

> *The knowledge that by means of work man shares in the work of creation constitutes the most profound motive for undertaking it in various sectors. The faithful, therefore… must learn the deepest meaning and the value of all creation, and its orientation to the praise of God. Even by their secular activity they must assist one another to live holier lives. In this way the world will be permeated by the spirit of Christ and more effectively achieve its purpose in justice, charity and peace.... Therefore, by their competence in secular fields and by their personal activity, elevated from within by the grace of Christ, let them work vigorously so that by human labor, technical skill, and civil culture created goods may be perfected according to the design of the Creator and the light of his Word.*[32]

When you are writing up a report, or fixing a drain, or washing dishes, or designing a skyscraper, or researching new energy sources—whatever form of human work you are engaged in—it is an opportunity for evangelizing the world, that it may be "permeated by the spirit of Christ and more effectively achieve its purpose." To elevate earthly activities, even the most mundane, to this level requires nothing more than infusing it with the "profound motive" our faith offers us, and thus orienting it to the praise of God. "Competence" and vigorous "personal activity" will be "elevated from within by the grace of Christ." Such is the noble vision God

---

32 St. John Paul II, *Laborem Exercens*, 25.

offers us for even the least-glamorous forms of human work. And that vision is what moves authentic Christians to fight against the petty, lazy tendencies of their fallen nature and pursue excellence in all they do.

The Patron Saint of Everybody

It is interesting to note that the patron saint of the Universal Church, St. Joseph, is also the patron saint of workers. In Scripture St. Joseph never speaks; he only works, obeying God's call to protect and provide for his family. This aspect of the human condition, the Church seems to be telling us, should never be belittled or overlooked. We truly can witness to God's love and Christ's truth by seeking faith-inspired excellence in our daily duties, which so often seem little more than trifles, and bothersome ones at that. If Jesus, Joseph, and Mary spent their lives among such trifles—and worked the world's redemption by doing so—then it's certainly okay for us to do so, too.

Questions for Personal Reflection or Group Discussion

1. What idea in this chapter struck you most and why?

2. How deeply do you feel the redemptive value of your normal work activities? What could you do to intensify your awareness of that value?

3. In which of your normal pursuits have you stopped seeking excellence? Why? In light of the ideas in this chapter, how do you think the Lord is inviting you to proceed in that area from now on?

4. St. Thérèse of Lisieux wrote, "What matters in life are not great deeds, but great love,"[33] and Blessed Mother Teresa of Calcutta

---

33 http://www.ncregister.com/daily-news/living-the-little-way-day-by-day.

used to say, "Not all of us can do great things. But we can do small things with great love."[34] Often we overlook the intrinsic value that our small actions have simply because we are God's children and therefore channels of grace in the world. What will you do today to better connect your daily work with your faith?

· When I feel frustrated or weighed down, I will invoke and try to enact the attitude contained in this verse from St. Paul: "Whatever you do, do from the heart, as for the Lord and not for others" (Colossians 3:23).

· I will begin and end today's least enjoyable task with a prayer.

· I will pause in the midst of today's chores and ask myself how I can do what I am doing better than I have done it in the past.

· (Write your own resolution) I will_____

Concluding Prayer

O God, Creator of all things,
who laid down for the human race the law of work,
graciously grant
that by the example of Saint Joseph and under his patronage
we may complete the works you set us to do
and attain the rewards you promise.
Through our Lord Jesus Christ, your Son,
who lives and reigns with you in the unity of the Holy Spirit,
one God, for ever and ever. Amen.

—*Roman Missal,* Collect for the Mass for May 1,
Feast of St. Joseph the Worker

---

34 http://www.goodreads.com/author/quotes/838305.Mother_Teresa.

Chapter 21
Your Way of Loving the Church

There is thus a profound link between Christ, the Church and evangelization. During the period of the Church that we are living in, it is she who has the task of evangelizing. This mandate is not accomplished without her, and still less against her.It is certainly fitting to recall this fact at a moment like the present one when it happens that not without sorrow we can hear people—whom we wish to believe are well-intentioned but who are certainly misguided in their attitude—continually claiming to love Christ but without the Church, to listen to Christ but not the Church, to belong to Christ but outside the Church. The absurdity of this dichotomy is clearly evident in this phrase of the gospel: "Anyone who rejects you rejects me." And how can one wish to love Christ without loving the Church, if the finest witness to Christ is that of St. Paul: "Christ loved the Church and sacrificed himself for her"?

—Blessed Paul VI, *Evangelii Nuntiandi,* 16

YOU, PERSONALLY, CANNOT save a single soul. Only God saves souls. Only God's grace redeems and renews the human heart, so wounded by original sin and all its consequences. Jesus is the source of that grace, and he has chosen to distribute it through his Church. The Church, guided and powered by the Holy Spirit, continues to proclaim the message of Jesus, translating that message into terms that can be grasped by each new generation and each new culture. The Church also imparts the sacraments, the objective signs and instruments of God's saving grace, in each individual life. Without the Church, who would guarantee the integrity of Christ's message through the vicissitudes of history? Who would keep the sacramental economy clicking?

Seed and Beginning of the Kingdom

The Church truly is the mother of Christians, both the origin and the goal of evangelization:

> *Henceforward the Church, endowed with the gifts of her founder and faithfully observing his precepts of charity, humility and self-denial, receives the mission of proclaiming and establishing among all peoples the Kingdom of Christ and of God, and she is on earth the seed and the beginning of that kingdom. (CCC, 768)*

For this reason, our apostolic witness necessarily includes showing a warm affection and supernatural reverence for the Church. The apostolate consists in bringing people closer and closer to Christ, for which the Church remains an irreplaceable mediator. We cannot pretend to be disciples and messengers of the Lord if at the same time we are indifferent or antagonistic to the Church. Blessed Pope Paul VI put this bluntly in his exhortation on evangelization:

> *[N]ot without sorrow we can hear people—whom we wish to believe are well-intentioned but who are certainly misguided in their attitude—continually claiming to love Christ but without the Church, to listen to Christ but not the Church, to belong to Christ but outside the Church.*[35]

---

35 Blessed Paul VI, *Evangelii Nuntiandi*, 16; http://w2.vatican.va/content/paul-vi/en/apost_exhortations/documents/hf_p-vi_exh_19751208_evangelii-nuntiandi.html.

Savoring the Sacraments

We bear witness to the Church's essential role in God's plan for the human family in many ways. Our own living of the sacraments and the liturgical year—which implies a conscientious and warm engagement in our local parish—is perhaps the most impactful. To quote Paul VI once again:

> To live the sacraments in this way, bringing their celebration to a true fullness, is not, as some would claim, to impede or to accept a distortion of evangelization: it is rather to complete it. For in its totality, evangelization— over and above the preaching of a message—consists in the implantation of the Church, which does not exist without the driving force which is the sacramental life culminating in the Eucharist.[36]

If the celebration of the Eucharist through the Holy Mass and devotion to the Eucharist through adoration of the Blessed Sacrament become pillars of our own personal and familial spirituality, that in itself will be a testimony to others (in addition to nourishing our own growth in spiritual maturity). If the confessional becomes a regular stop on our hectic journey through this fallen world, that too will overflow in surprising ways as a sign of God's presence and power to those who know and interact with us (in addition to flooding our hearts with fresh outpouring of God's redeeming mercy). Even the other sacraments, which we receive only once or, in the case of marriage and anointing of the sick, possibly more than once, can become beacons of Christian witness when we surround them with meaningful family traditions, joyfully celebrate their anniversaries, and intentionally seek to understand and activate their power in our lives.

---

36 Ibid., 28.

Living the Liturgical Year

It is similar with the rhythms of the liturgical year. When a Catholic family makes the liturgical year, as opposed to the civil year, the primary matrix of their weekly, monthly, and annual activities, they become living signs of the spiritual realm and the eternal truths. Sundays and other liturgical solemnities, saints' days, liturgical seasons (Advent, Christmas, Lent, Holy Week, Easter)—the Church offers us these tangible touch points in order to help us keep a truly spiritual, Christ-centered, heavenly trajectory to our lives. We ignore or belittle them (treating Sunday as a normal day, for example) at our own risk, and at the risk of blending in to the secularized culture so much that our Christian witness is watered down, if not completely compromised.

Studying and therefore understanding and knowing how to explain the teachings of the Church (instead of arrogantly setting up our own opinions as a kind of parallel magisterium) is another form of the apostolate of witness. Just as we would expect a medical doctor to be able to speak intelligently, interestingly, and definitively about his or her area of medical expertise, so too unbelievers rightly expect that a self-proclaimed Catholic Christian should be able to do the same regarding the Church's doctrine in relation to faith and morals. Not that every Catholic is called to become a professional theologian, but every Catholic should seek to be well-versed enough in the faith to represent it fairly and warmly when the need or opportunity arises.

Poisoning the Well

Perhaps the most common way this area of witness breaks down has to do with useless criticism. We all know that the Church, though divine in its origin and in the means by which it carries out its mission, is also human. It is made up of sinners. As a result members of the Church always have plenty of things to complain about. And yet those complaints, as legitimate as they may be, can easily undermine our testimony to the deeper reality of the Church.

God doesn't need the human side of the Church to be perfect in order to continue his flow of grace into the world. Endless complaining and destructive criticism seem to suppose that he does. Instead of falling into those sterile behaviors, we should follow God's own example of mercy and invest our energies in positive action— taking the initiative to help fix what needs to be fixed, disciplining our own attitudes and words so that any criticism we might have is constructive, and recognizing and speaking freely about the amazing good God works through the Church. That will better help open peoples' eyes to the grace that awaits them therein.

In short, by loving the Church, wrinkles and all, we will naturally stimulate interest and curiosity on behalf of those who are outside the Church, giving God's providence plenty of opportunities to open hearts and minds that have long been closed to the love of the Lord. This too is part of the apostolate we can pursue simply by the way we live our daily lives.

Questions for Personal Reflection or Group Discussion

1. What idea in this chapter struck you most and why?

2. How would you describe your engagement with your local parish? How could you improve it?

3. What aspects of the Church do you complain about most often? How helpful are your complaints for your own spiritual growth? How would you describe the difference between useless whining, patient acceptance, and constructive action?

4. Every Catholic family is in a sense a domestic church—a mini Catholic community called to reflect and embody the life and mission of the universal Church in its own milieu. The activities of the universal Church, therefore, should in some form be

present in this domestic church: prayer, study, fellowship, mutual service, mission, and so on. What will you do today to help develop your domestic church?

- I will place an inspiring Catholic image (crucifix, picture of the Blessed Virgin Mary, picture of a saint, etc.) in my own room, so as to foster a more prayerful attitude when I am alone and engaged in my personal activities.

- I will put an image of the Sacred Heart of Jesus and a candle in a visible area of our home (living room, family room, foyer) as a way of giving testimony to our faith and tangibly consecrating our family to God's service. (If you like this idea, you might want to read about the tradition of Enthroning the Sacred Heart in the home; see sacredheartapostolate.com.)

- I will renew our family's commitment to pray together, at the very least by praying grace before meals.

- (Write your own resolution) I will_____

Concluding Prayer

We thank you, Lord Jesus, because the gospel of the Father's love, with which you came to save the world, has been proclaimed far and wide in the world as a gift of the Holy Spirit that fills us with gladness.

We thank you for the gift of your life, which you have given us by loving us to the end: your life makes us children of God, brothers and sisters to each other.

Increase, O Lord, our faith and our love for you, present in every tabernacle. Grant us to be faithful witnesses to your resurrection to all people, especially the youth, so that, in knowing you, they may follow you and find in you their peace and joy. Only then will they know that they are brothers and sisters of all God's children scattered throughout the world.

*You who, in becoming man, chose to belong to a human family,
teach families the virtues which filled with light the family home
of Nazareth. May families always be united, as you and the Father
are one, and may they be living witnesses to love, justice and
solidarity; make them schools of respect, forgiveness and mutual
help, so that the world may believe; help them to be the source of
vocations to the priesthood and the consecrated life, and all the
other forms of firm Christian commitment.*

*Protect your Church and the successor of Peter, to whom you,
Good Shepherd, have entrusted the task of feeding your flock.
Teach us to love your Mother, Mary, as you love her. Give us
strength to proclaim your Word with courage in the work of the
new evangelization, so that the world may know new hope.
Mary, Mother of the Church, pray for us!*

—Adapted from St. John Paul II's prayer at the end of *Ecclesia in
America*, January, 22, 1999[37]

---

37 http://w2.vatican.va/content/john-paul-ii/en/apost_exhortations/
documents/hf_jp-ii_exh_22011999_ecclesia-in-america.html.

Chapter 22
Speaking the Words of Life

*Nevertheless this [witness] always remains insufficient, because
even the finest witness will prove ineffective in the long run if it is not
explained, justified—what Peter called always having "your answer
ready for people who ask you the reason for the hope that you all
have" (1 Peter 3:15)—and made explicit by a clear and unequivocal
proclamation of the Lord Jesus. The Good News proclaimed by the
witness of life sooner or later has to be proclaimed by the word
of life. There is no true evangelization if the name, the teaching,
the life, the promises, the kingdom and the mystery of Jesus of
Nazareth, the Son of God are not proclaimed.*

—Blessed Paul VI, *Evangelii Nuntiandi*, 22 (emphasis added)

IF YOU HAD discovered the cure for cancer, the truly loving thing
to do would be to share that discovery with those who suffer from
the disease. Even if the cure were bitter and painful, keeping it to
yourself for fear of offending a cancer victim who may resent the
bitterness of the pill would be a lack of love, a self-centered and
vain pretension.

Jesus Is the Cure

This seems so obvious. And yet, when it comes to spiritual diseases
and spiritual cures, the obvious sometimes gets obscured. Jesus
Christ truly is the cure for life's moral and spiritual ills. As we

have seen, his teaching, preserved and communicated in every generation by the Church, points the way to healthy and happy living: "I am the light of the world. Whoever follows me will not walk in darkness, but will have the light of life" (John 8:12). To know him, accept him, and follow him opens the door to the interior freedom and fulfillment we all yearn for: "If you remain in my word, you will truly be my disciples, and you will know the truth, and the truth will set you free" (John 8:31–32).

He is not only one worthy figure among the world's great philosophers; he is not only one respectable founder among history's great founders of religion; he is not only one wise teacher among humanity's top gurus: he is the incarnate Son of God, the second Person of the Holy Trinity become man; the sole Savior of the world.

"I am the way and the truth and the life. No one comes to the Father except through me.…" There is no salvation through anyone else, nor is there any other name under heaven given to the human race by which we are to be saved. (John 14:6; Acts 4:12)

People searching for happiness, inner peace, and meaning are searching for Jesus, whether they realize it or not. He is the cure— the only cure—for their spiritual diseases, which can be immensely painful and debilitating even for people who seem to be doing pretty well by all external appearances.

You Have the Cure

Only Jesus can forgive sins and heal the wounds caused by sin. Only Jesus can give the answers to the deepest questions of the human heart. Only his teaching provides sure guidance through the confused, maddening moral labyrinths of the post-modern world. And you know him. You believe in him. You are familiar with those teachings. You have the cure for your neighbor's spiritual ills—will you keep it to yourself?

We cannot force people to accept Jesus and his teachings, but we are called to tell people about him. If we don't, some of those people in our circles of influence may never even be given the chance to put their faith in the Lord:

For "everyone who calls on the name of the Lord will be saved." But how can they call on him in whom they have not believed? And how can they believe in him of whom they have not heard? And how can they hear without someone to preach? (Romans 13:14)

Telling people about Jesus, sharing the gospel with them, explaining the reasons behind the moral and theological tenets of Christianity—this is a fundamental dimension of every Christian's mission, a central way to "love your neighbor as yourself" and exercise the prophetic facet of our Christian vocation.

Delivering the Message

The first dimension of mission (which we have been reflecting on in the previous chapters) has to do with our way of daily living, the witness of our own moral integrity, love for the Church, and pursuit of excellence. And that is, in many cases, a necessary precursor to effectively speaking the words of life—people will tend to listen to what we say with a more open mind if they have seen us behave admirably beforehand.

But at times God also nudges us to speak about him regardless of the relationship we have with a person. Sometimes, in other words, he wants us to take the initiative and bring up the topic of religion. We need to be ready and willing to do that. More often, perhaps, we need to be ready to respond to questions that are asked of us directly or that come up indirectly in conversations. We need to know how to express and explain what we believe, and we need to cultivate the courage—based on true love for our neighbor—to do so when the need or opportunity arises.

That requires doing our homework. We can never have all the answers to every question or objection, but we can gradually increase our knowledge and understanding of the faith so as to be better and better at explaining it. A good rule of thumb is to try to avoid having to say, "I am not sure how to answer that" more than once. When someone brings up a question you can't answer, make a commitment to investigate and study until you *can* answer it, so that the next time it comes up, you will able to shed God's light on it.

Our Manner Affects Our Message

Of course, the manner in which we speak about Jesus and his teachings is almost as important as the content of what we say. If our manner lacks respect and humility, our words will simply go unheard. Timing matters. Tone matters. Attitude matters. It is not primarily about winning arguments and making converts in order to feed our vanity—it is about loving our neighbors as ourselves, sharing with them the good news we have received from others. We are simply heralds of Christ's message, ambassadors of his kingdom, and so our egos don't have to get involved. "Whoever listens to you listens to me," Jesus pointed out. "Whoever rejects you rejects me. And whoever rejects me rejects the one who sent me" (Luke 10:16).

True love seeks ways to communicate the truth that truly saves—it doesn't cop out by throwing up its hands and saying, "Whatever you want to do and believe is perfectly fine with me." That's now how Jesus fulfilled his redeeming mission of love, and it's not how we should live our mission, either.

Questions for Personal Reflection or Group Discussion

1. What idea in this chapter struck you most and why?

2. How well do you know your faith? Could you explain the gospel to someone who asked you to? What are you doing to

continue deepening your knowledge and your ability to share that knowledge with others?

3. How well do you understand the reasons behind the Church's moral teachings, which are so maligned in today's world? Which ones are you most comfortable talking about? Which ones are you least comfortable talking about? Why?

4. Fear often inhibits us from speaking about what we believe and why. We are afraid of being labeled a fanatic; we are afraid of being rejected; we are afraid of being made fun of or persecuted in some way; we are afraid of being humiliated if we can't hold up our side of an argument. And yet Jesus himself experienced all of those things in response to his saving mission—he was rejected, humiliated, and persecuted even though his knowledge and love were perfect. What will you do today to overcome your fear of sharing the faith?

• I will publicly display some sign that I am a Christian (a necklace with a cross on it, a rosary bracelet, etc.).

• I will begin researching one of the questions about my faith I don't feel comfortable answering.

• I will find a good Catholic radio station or podcast to start listening to on a regular basis in order to better equip myself for my mission of speaking about the gospel.

• (Write your own resolution) I will_____

Concluding Prayer

Mary, Virgin and Mother, you who, moved by the Holy Spirit, welcomed the word of life in the depths of your humble faith: as you gave yourself completely to the Eternal One, help us to say our own "yes" to the urgent call, as pressing as ever, to proclaim the good news of Jesus.

Obtain for us now a new ardor born of the resurrection, that we may bring to all the gospel of life which triumphs over death. Give us a holy courage to seek new paths, that the gift of unfading beauty may reach every man and woman.

Virgin of listening and contemplation, Mother of love, Bride of the eternal wedding feast, pray for the Church, whose pure icon you are, that she may never be closed in on herself or lose her passion for establishing God's kingdom.

Star of the new evangelization, help us to bear radiant witness to communion, service, ardent and generous faith, justice and love of the poor, that the joy of the Gospel may reach to the ends of the earth, illuminating even the fringes of our world.

Mother of the living gospel, wellspring of happiness for God's little ones, pray for us.

Amen. Alleluia!

—Pope Francis, *Evangelii Gaudium*, 288

Chapter 23
Your Works of Mercy

The scenario of poverty can extend indefinitely, if in addition to its traditional forms we think of its newer patterns. These latter often affect financially affluent sectors and groups which are nevertheless threatened by despair at the lack of meaning in their lives, by drug addiction, by fear of abandonment in old age or sickness, by marginalization or social discrimination. In this context Christians must learn to make their act of faith in Christ by discerning his voice in the cry for help that rises from this world of poverty. This means carrying on the tradition of charity which has expressed itself in so many different ways in the past two millennia, but which today calls for even greater resourcefulness. Now is the time for a new "creativity" in charity, not only by ensuring that help is effective but also by "getting close" to those who suffer, so that the hand that helps is seen not as a humiliating handout but as a sharing between brothers and sisters.

—St. John Paul II, *Novo Millennio Ineunte*, 50

BY OUR WAY of living—our example of striving for moral integrity, acting with kindness, talking like a Christian, loving the Church, and humbly pursuing excellence in everything we do—we give witness to God's goodness and love. That is our apostolate of testimony, by which our lives take on a priestly meaning and bring this fallen world back into communion with God. By proclaiming and explaining the person and message of Jesus with our words, we exercise the prophetic dimension of our Christian vocation and engage in apostolate through a verbal witness to God's truth and love (we explored that in the last chapter). The third mode of apostolate, an expression of the kingly dimension of our vocation as Christ's followers, has to do with our Christian works: specific actions and ongoing projects that "impregnate culture and human works with a moral value."[38]

The Power of Mercy

The first arena of these works is the most basic, and it has to do with actively helping people who are in need. In a certain sense, this is the most obvious expression of obedience to Our Lord's command: "Love your neighbor as yourself.... Do to others whatever you would have them do to you" (Matthew 22:39, 7:12).

The Church's long and fruitful tradition of spirituality helps make this basic criteria more concrete by identifying two categories of actions that embody this Christlike, self-giving love: the corporal works of mercy and the spiritual works of mercy.

In biblical language, the term *mercy* refers to the generous love God has never ceased showing to the human family ever since sin entered the world. Mercy is love that reaches out to serve those who are suffering and in need regardless of whether they deserve, strictly speaking, to receive such service. St. John Paul II described it vividly when he wrote about Jesus himself as the incarnation of God's mercy:

> *Especially through his lifestyle and through his actions, Jesus revealed that love is present in the world in which we live—an effective love, a love that addresses itself to man and embraces everything that makes up his humanity. This love makes itself particularly noticed in contact with*

---

38 The Second Vatican Council, *Apostolicam Actuositatem*, 7; *CCC*, 909.

suffering, injustice and poverty—in contact with the whole historical "human condition," which in various ways manifests man's limitation and frailty, both physical and moral. It is precisely the mode and sphere in which love manifests itself that in biblical language is called "mercy."[39]

Christ's Standard for Christian Behavior

The corporal and spiritual works of mercy, then, are ways of continuing Christ's own loving mission by making love "present in the world…particularly noticed in contact with suffering, injustice, and poverty.…" In fact, toward the end of his public life, Jesus revealed that the quality of our Christian life is inextricably intertwined with the extent to which we engage in works of mercy. Through his incarnation Jesus has mysteriously but truly identified himself with every human person, and so the way we treat neighbors in need directly manifests the depth of our love for the Lord.

"Then the king will say to those on his right, 'Come, you who are blessed by my Father. Inherit the kingdom prepared for you from the foundation of the world. For I was hungry and you gave me food, I was thirsty and you gave me drink, a stranger and you welcomed me, naked and you clothed me, ill and you cared for me, in prison and you visited me.' Then the righteous will answer him and say, 'Lord, when did we see you hungry and feed you, or thirsty and give you drink? When did we see you a stranger and welcome you, or naked and clothe you? When did we see you ill or in prison, and visit you?' And the king will say to them in reply, 'Amen, I say to you, whatever you did for one of these least brothers of mine, you did for me.'"
(Matthew 25:34–40)

---

39 St. John Paul II, *Dives in Misercordia*, 3.

Our example of Christian living and our willingness to speak of Christ to those who don't know him or who resist him must overflow into a practical generosity and spirit of service. Otherwise our love remains immature.

St. James picked up on this theme in a famous passage where he illustrates the obvious, emphasizing that faith—true belief in Jesus and his message—by its very nature overflows into works:

For the judgment is merciless to one who has not shown mercy…. What good is it, my brothers, if someone says he has faith but does not have works? Can that faith save him? If a brother or sister has nothing to wear and has no food for the day, and one of you says to them, "Go in peace, keep warm, and eat well," but you do not give them the necessities of the body, what good is it? So also faith of itself, if it does not have works, is dead. (James 2:13–17)

Another of the twelve apostles, St. John, put it even more succinctly, linking the Christian behavior of practical service to the example of Jesus that inspires it:

The way we came to know love was that he laid down his life for us; so we ought to lay down our lives for our brothers. If someone who has worldly means sees a brother in need and refuses him compassion, how can the love of God remain in him? Children, let us love not in word or speech but in deed and truth. (1 John 3:16–18)

All these passages point in the same direction: Claiming to love God while refusing to reach out and help a neighbor in need when we can is a form of hypocrisy. It constitutes the sin of omission, the sin of omitting to do the worthy (and sometimes necessary) good within our reach.

What Are the "Works of Mercy"?

The *Catechism* lists the traditional works of mercy in order to make the commandment of neighborly love practical, to help us keep in mind and stay sensitive to the most common needs that our neighbors experience. It points out that the list is only indicative, not exhaustive.

> *The works of mercy are charitable actions by which we come to the aid of our neighbor in his spiritual and bodily necessities. Instructing, advising, consoling, comforting are spiritual works of mercy, as are forgiving and bearing wrongs patiently.*[40] *The corporal works of mercy consist especially in feeding the hungry, sheltering the homeless, clothing the naked, visiting the sick and imprisoned, and burying the dead. Among all these, giving alms to the poor is one of the chief witnesses to fraternal charity: it is also a work of justice pleasing to God. (CCC, 2447, emphasis added).*

We don't have to travel far to find ways to engage in these works— our own living rooms, backyards, and neighborhoods are the right place to start. The important thing is to cultivate the attitude of care, concern, and attentiveness that keeps us aware of the needs those around us may have so we form a habit of living on the wavelength of mercy: "Blessed are the merciful, for they will be shown mercy" (Matthew 5:7).

As that habit forms, we will also become more docile to the inspirations of the Holy Spirit, which often invite individual Christians to create projects and institutions that can serve these needs on a large scale. Such initiatives—from orphanages to hospitals, from schools to treatment centers, from international humanitarian networks to entire religious orders dedicated to

---

40 Traditionally, a seventh work of mercy completes this list: *praying for the living and the dead.*

serving persecuted Christians—have always blossomed wherever the Church is alive and well.

Whether in day-to-day interactions or vast institutional efforts, the works of mercy remain the most fundamental form of the apostolate linked to the third W (after *way* and *words*): our *works*.

Questions for Personal Reflection or Group Discussion

1. What idea in this chapter struck you most and why?

2. How would you explain the Christian concept of "mercy" in your own words? What are some of the most common misunderstandings or misuses of this term, in your experience?

3. Pope Benedict XVI offered a theological reflection on the connection between seeking our own salvation and seeking the salvation of those around us. He wrote:

    "The lives of others continually spill over into mine: in what I think, say, do and achieve. And conversely, my life spills over into that of others: for better and for worse.... As Christians we should never limit ourselves to asking: how can I save myself? We should also ask: what can I do in order that others may be saved and that for them too the star of hope may rise? Then I will have done my utmost for my own personal salvation as well."[41]

4. What do you think he means by this—what is the deeper connection between our own personal salvation and our efforts to help those around us? How does that apply to your own life?

5. Sometimes we can feel overwhelmed by the sheer quantity of need being experienced by the human family. We feel so small

---

41 Benedict XVI, *Spe Salvi*, #48.

and helpless in the face of it. *What can I do to stem that tide?* we find ourselves objecting. Blessed Mother Teresa of Calcutta once responded to a question like that by saying, "Pick up a broom." What do you think she meant by that?

6. What it would look like today if you were to "pick up a broom" in your own life?

7. What arena of basic human need moves your heart most? Have you ever thought that this special sensitivity may be a hidden call from the Lord to become more actively engaged in a specific type of merciful work? Think about it, prayerfully, right now.

Concluding Prayer

Father, by the power of the Spirit,
strengthen the Church's commitment
to the new evangelization
and guide our steps along the pathways of the world,
to proclaim Christ by our lives,
and to direct our earthly pilgrimage
toward the City of heavenly light.
May Christ's followers show forth their love
for the poor and the oppressed;
may they be one with those in need
and abound in works of mercy;
may they be compassionate toward all,
that they themselves may obtain indulgence
and forgiveness from you.
Praise and glory to You, Most Holy Trinity, you alone are
God most high!

—St. John Paul II, Prayer for the Celebration of the
Great Jubilee of the Year 2000[42]

---

42 http://w2.vatican.va/content/john-paul-ii/en/prayers/documents/hf_
jp-ii_1999_jub-prayer-padre.html.

Chapter 24
Renewing the Fabric of Society

Lay people, whose particular vocation places them in the midst of the world and in charge of the most varied temporal tasks, must for this very reason exercise a very special form of evangelization.

Their primary and immediate task is not to establish and develop the ecclesial community—this is the specific role of the pastors—but to put to use every Christian and evangelical possibility latent but already present and active in the affairs of the world. Their own field of evangelizing activity is the vast and complicated world of politics, society and economics, but also the world of culture, of the sciences and the arts, of international life, of the mass media. It also includes other realities which are open to evangelization, such as human love, the family, the education of children and adolescents, professional work, suffering. The more gospel-inspired lay people there are engaged in these realities, clearly involved in them, competent to promote them and conscious that they must exercise to the full their Christian powers which are often buried and suffocated, the more these realities will be at the service of the kingdom of God and therefore of salvation in Jesus Christ, without in any way losing or sacrificing their human content but rather pointing to a transcendent dimension which is often disregarded.

—Blessed Paul VI, *Evangelii Nuntiandi,* 70

THE GOAL OF the apostolate, the goal of the Church's evangelization efforts, is to bring and constantly deepen the reign of Christ *everywhere*—into every human heart, family, community, and culture. We seek nothing less than to infuse every human reality with the redeeming truth of Christ's message and the redeeming power of Christ's grace. In Jesus's commissioning of his Church to fulfill that mission, notice the universal scope, the unlimited boundaries of his vision:

> *"Go, therefore, and make disciples of all nations, baptizing them in the name of the Father, and of the Son, and of the holy Spirit, teaching them to observe all that I have commanded you." (Matthew 28:19–20, emphasis added)*

All nations are to become disciples; *all* that Jesus taught and commanded is to be known, loved, and followed by *everyone.* That's the work of evangelization. That's our mission.

Transforming Humanity from Within

Blessed Paul VI described this ambitious and energizing goal in more existential terms:

> *For the Church, evangelizing means bringing the Good News into all the strata of humanity, and through its influence transforming humanity from within and making it new…. The purpose of evangelization is therefore precisely this interior change, and if it had to be expressed in one sentence the best way of stating it would be to say that the Church evangelizes when she seeks to convert, solely through the divine power of the message she proclaims, both the personal and collective consciences of people, the activities in which they engage, and the lives and concrete milieu which are theirs…. All this could be expressed in the following words: what matters is to evangelize man's culture and cultures (not in a purely decorative way, as it*

were, by applying a thin veneer, but in a vital way, in depth and right to their very roots).[43]

Jesus used a simple image to describe this process of cultural transformation when he explained the nature of his kingdom: "He spoke to them another parable. 'The kingdom of heaven is like yeast that a woman took and mixed with three measures of wheat flour until the whole batch was leavened'" (Matthew 13:33).

Not Just a Pipe Dream

The development of western civilization in the Christian era demonstrates that this mission is more than a fairy tale. Greco-Roman civilization and Anglo-Germanic culture were both penetrated and transformed by the Christian ethos, creating a new culture. Over the course of a thousand years, the previously pagan scale of values was overturned by the influence of the gospel and its message of human dignity, divine mercy, and everlasting life. The institutions of European society developed under this spiritual tutorship, spreading wherever the Christians went to explore and to build. Many of the ideas found in the gospel were foreign and even contradictory to much of what the Greco-Roman and Germanic peoples adhered to. Concepts like humility and celibacy, care for the poor and inter-communitary justice (equality of human rights), and natural moral law were only vaguely present in pre-Christian worldviews, if they were present at all. Through the work and lives of Christians, they came to become common presuppositions in Western mentalities and legal systems. This led to flourishing achievements in every field of human endeavor, including science and technology, education, literature and the arts, and even politics and economics.

Certainly it wasn't heaven on earth, as some Western civilization apologists like to claim. In fact Jesus had promised it would never

---

43 Blessed Paul VI, *Evangelii Nuntiandi*, 18, 20 (emphasis added).

be so until his second coming. In the parable of the wheat and the weeds, he promised that good and bad would grow up side by side throughout the history of his Church, and the full purification from evil would only occur at the end of the earthly story:

"He who sows good seed is the Son of Man, the field is the world, the good seed the children of the kingdom. The weeds are the children of the evil one, and the enemy who sows them is the devil. The harvest is the end of the age, and the harvesters are angels. Just as weeds are collected and burned [up] with fire, so will it be at the end of the age. The Son of Man will send his angels, and they will collect out of his kingdom all who cause others to sin and all evildoers. They will throw them into the fiery furnace, where there will be wailing and grinding of teeth. Then the righteous will shine like the sun in the kingdom of their Father." (Matthew 13:37–43)

But just as the weeds are real, so is the wheat. And the call to penetrate all human affairs with the good yeast of the gospel is still valid, still an essential aspect of our evangelizing mission.

God's Ambassadors to Every Sector of Society

God calls all of us to share in this aspect, too. The first Christians didn't hunker down and go into hiding in the face of ancient Rome's aggressive, anti-Christian paganism. Yes, they prudently guarded their worship services and formation activities from prying eyes in order to avoid unnecessary trouble, but at the same time they brought their faith to bear on the world in which they lived. They believed in the power of Christ's message to transform the milieus in which they lived and worked.

Christian philosophers challenged and dialogued with pagan philosophers. Christian soldiers courageously imbued their military service with honor and moral integrity. Christian families rescued infants legally abandoned in forest clearings outside the city limits. Christian merchants and politicians battled corruption and worked to transform legal structures and economic customs in harmony with the true common good. Christian doctors and teachers defended moral truth and created new institutions dedicated to serving the underprivileged as well as those who could pay. In short, every sphere of society was penetrated not by "the Church" in the abstract, but by individual Christians whom God endowed and called to be missionaries within particular branches of human endeavor.

The new evangelization must include this same dimension; it must follow this same pattern. Imagine how different our culture would be if every Catholic—or even one in every ten Catholics— was fully aware and fully engaged in this kind of effort. We have no cause to wait for "the Church" to Christianize culture; we *are* the Church wherever we work and live. And we are present in every nook and cranny of society. God is eager to give us the courage and wisdom to proclaim and build up Christ's kingdom right there. We just need to seize the opportunities, to believe, and to launch ourselves into the fray. If we don't, who will?

The split between the gospel and culture is without a doubt the drama of our time, just as it was of other times. Therefore every effort must be made to ensure a full evangelization of culture, or more correctly of cultures. They have to be regenerated by an encounter with the gospel.[44]

Questions for Personal Reflection or Group Discussion

1. What idea in this chapter struck you most and why?

2. How firmly do you believe that Jesus really wants to convert the

---

44 Ibid., 20 (emphasis added).

entire world, every single person? How firmly do you believe that he wants to work through you to help achieve that goal?

3. How can you better infuse gospel values in your workplace or other circles of influence with cultural implications?

4. God calls all of us to bring the gospel into the circles of society where we live and work, through our way of being, our words, and our works. And to do so, he endows each of us with certain talents and gifts. What will you do today to use your personal gifts for God's glory and to further the Church's work of evangelization?

• I will sit down with a friend and ask him or her to help me identify my top three or four personal gifts.

• I will spend some time prayerfully reflecting on the strong desires in my heart—desires to take on a particular project or get involved in a certain type of apostolic activity, desires that have been resonating in my heart and may be indicating an invitation from the Lord, but which I haven't yet responded to. I will write these down and ask God to show me how to take the next step.

• I will remember the idealistic dreams of doing something great for God that motivated me in the past, and I will prayerfully reflect on what role those dreams should still be playing in my life now.

• (Write your own reflection) I will_____

Concluding Prayer

I am created to do something or to be something for which no one else is created; I have a place in God's counsels, in God's world, which no one else has; whether I be rich or poor, despised or esteemed by man, God knows me and calls me by my name.

God has created me to do Him some definite service; He has committed some work to me which He has not committed to another. I have my mission—I never may know it in this life, but I shall be told it in the next. Somehow I am necessary for His purposes, as necessary in my place as an Archangel in his—if, indeed, I fail, He can raise another, as He could make the stones children of Abraham. Yet I have a part in this great work; I am a link in a chain, a bond of connection between persons. He has not created me for naught. I shall do good, I shall do His work; I shall be an angel of peace, a preacher of truth in my own place, while not intending it, if I do but keep His commandments and serve Him in my calling.

Therefore I will trust Him. Whatever, wherever I am, I can never be thrown away. If I am in sickness, my sickness may serve Him; in perplexity, my perplexity may serve Him; if I am in sorrow, my sorrow may serve Him. My sickness, or perplexity, or sorrow may be necessary causes of some great end, which is quite beyond us. He does nothing in vain; He may prolong my life, He may shorten it; He knows what He is about. He may take away my friends, He may throw me among strangers, He may make me feel desolate, make my spirits sink, hide the future from me—still He knows what He is about.

—Blessed John Henry Newman[45]

---

45 http://www.newmanreader.org/works/meditations/meditations9.html

Chapter 25
Relationships or Activities?

It is not therefore a matter of inventing a "new program." The program already exists: it is the plan found in the gospel and in the living Tradition, it is the same as ever. Ultimately, it has its center in Christ himself, who is to be known, loved and imitated, so that in him we may live the life of the Trinity, and with him transform history until its fulfillment in the heavenly Jerusalem. This is a program which does not change with shifts of times and cultures, even though it takes account of time and culture for the sake of true dialogue and effective communication. This program for all times is our program.

—St. John Paul II, *Novo Millennio Ineunte,* 29

THE INSTRUCTIONS JESUS gave when he sent out the first Christian missionaries included a curious directive: "Whatever town or village you enter, look for a worthy person in it, and stay there until you leave"(Matthew 10:11).

Christian Mission Is about People

The implication is clear: Mission, for a Christian, is primarily about people. The whole history of salvation follows this same pattern. God begins to unfold his plan of redemption by establishing a relationship with the chosen people of Israel, and this relationship becomes the central characteristic of Israel's very identity.

> *I will take you as my own people, and I will be your God…. Ever present in your midst, I will be your God, and you will be my people…. You shall be my people, and I will be your God.* (Exodus 6:7; Leviticus 26:12; Jeremiah 30:22)

Through the Incarnation, God elevates his relationship with us to a shocking new level. By taking on human nature, he enables us to interact with him just as we interact with any human friend: "I no longer call you slaves, because a slave does not know what his master is doing. I have called you friends, because I have told you everything I have heard from my Father" (John 15:15).

Original sin shattered a relationship of trust between God and the human family: "Man, tempted by the devil, let his trust in his Creator die in his heart" (*CCC*, 397). God originally established that relationship to be the source of meaning and joy for human beings: "Man was made to live in communion with God, in whom he finds happiness" (*CCC*, 45). And so it makes perfect sense that God's plan for redeeming us from sin involves reestablishing a real, interpersonal relationship with the human family and each member of it, not simply tweaking a damaged social system or repairing a technical malfunction.

The Real Meaning of Religion

Whenever we forget the centrality of relationship in the Christian worldview, we play into the hands of critics and cynics who consider religion to be nothing more than empty rituals and soulless formalities. We all know people who have left the Church because of this. They learned how to make the Sign of the Cross; they learned a few answers to questions in *Catechism* classes; they learned when to stand and sit and kneel during Mass; but they never experienced a personal encounter with God. Jesus remained for them a shadowy historical figure, not a real person passionately interested in their lives.

Developing a personal relationship with God in the context of a community of believers who make up the family of God—this is the real core of true religion. Making this possible was a central part of the radical, revolutionary message of Jesus Christ.

And so, as we strive to find creative ways to spread that message, we have to give priority to relationships. Otherwise we will end up betraying the very idea we are trying to communicate. Jesus commanded us to "love your neighbor as yourself" (Matthew 22:39). Love means relationship, personal investment, interpersonal knowledge, and mutual esteem. To be Christ's messengers to the world, his apostles and missionaries, requires us to care enough about the people whom Jesus came to save that we are willing to become vulnerable and enter into relationship with them: "Whatever town or village you enter, look for a worthy person in it, and stay there until you leave" (Matthew 10:11).

Beyond Techniques

Any apostolic activity we engage in should include, or at least be open to, this dimension. Christianity is not a technique that people can learn and apply with clinical precision. Christianity is a network of faith-based relationships that flows outward from a personal encounter with the one, true, Triune God—Father, Son, and Holy Spirit—who *is* relationship and requires relationship: "Whoever is without love does not know God, for God is love" (1 John 4:8). Our apostolic endeavors have to be conceived and executed from that perspective.

Apostolates like camps, schools, Bible studies, service projects, publishing houses, websites, hospitals, professional associations, conferences, radio shows, formation programs, and even whole parishes are never ends in themselves. Rather, every apostolate is an effort to create an environment or situation in which personal encounters with Christ and among actual or potential members of the Body of Christ have a better chance of happening and flourishing. Apostolic activities are meant to be catalysts that initiate or deepen Christian experience, which is always in some way an experience of God and God's family.

Avoiding a Tricky Idolatry

And so we must resist the temptation to idolize our apostolates, as if the perfect apostolate will be able to conquer evil and usher in a new Golden Age of Christianity. There is no Golden Age, and there never has been. Every period in the history of the Church has had its crises as well as its saints. The age in which we live is no exception. Our Christian mission spurs us on to find creative ways to evangelize, to come up with new apostolates that can expand the reach—both in breadth and in depth—of Christ's message in our world, but in the end they are merely tools. The real heart of evangelization is found not in perfect pastoral programs or killer apps, which are merely useful instruments, but in relationships of love—love for Christ and love for neighbor.

Pope Benedict XVI put this beautifully in his very first encyclical letter, *God Is Love*:

> *Love of neighbor is thus shown to be possible in the way proclaimed by the Bible, by Jesus. It consists in the very fact that, in God and with God, I love even the person whom I do not like or even know. This can only take place on the basis of an intimate encounter with God, an encounter which has become a communion of will, even affecting my feelings. Then I learn to look on this other person not simply with my eyes and my feelings, but from the perspective of Jesus Christ. His friend is my friend. Going beyond exterior appearances, I perceive in others an interior desire for a sign of love, of concern. This I can offer them not only through the organizations intended for such purposes, accepting it perhaps as a political necessity. Seeing with the eyes of Christ, I can give to others much more than*

their outward necessities; I can give them the look of love which they crave.[46]

"His friend is my friend"—this is the heart of apostolic activity. I want to give to others what Jesus has given to me, and I want to do so because Jesus wants me to. Evangelization is never mechanical; it is never technocratic. It is about people, and relationships, and the living God who is present in all of them.

All people desire to leave a lasting mark. But what endures? Money does not. Even buildings do not, nor books. After a certain time, longer or shorter, all these things disappear. The only thing that lasts forever is the human soul, the human person created by God for eternity.... It is here that appears the dynamism of the life of a Christian, an apostle: I chose you to go forth. We must be enlivened by a holy restlessness: a restlessness to bring to everyone the gift of faith, of friendship with Christ. Truly, the love and friendship of God was given to us so that it might also be shared with others. We have received the faith to give it to others.... And we must bear fruit that will endure.[47]

Questions for Personal Reflection or Group Discussion

1. What idea in this chapter struck you most and why?

2. Considering the reflections in this chapter, what do you think is the best way to evaluate the effectiveness of our apostolic activities?

3. What would you say to someone who wanted to come up with creative means of evangelization to reach as many people as possible? Could an inspiration like that—so focused on visible

---

46 Pope Benedict XVI, *Deus Caritas Est,* 18.
47 Joseph Cardinal Ratzinger, homily, April 18, 2005; http://www.vatican.va/ gpll/documents/homily-pro-eligendo-pontifice_20050418_en.html.

results and measurable numbers—come from the Holy Spirit? Why or why not?

4. Throughout this book, we have explained that apostolic action can take three forms: the priestly form of living our daily activities as an offering to God and thereby as a witness to his goodness; the prophetic form of telling people about Jesus and his message; and the kingly form of working to transform society in accordance with God's plan. In your own life, which of those three is in the best condition and why? What will you do today to make an improvement in the one that needs it most?

- I will seek advice from someone I trust about an aspect of my life I have been uncomfortable with for a while.
- I will bring up religion in a normal conversation and see where it goes.
- I will visit my parish or diocesan website and look for opportunities to volunteer my time in some apostolic activity during the coming weeks.
- (Write your own resolution) I will_____

Concluding Prayer

Dear Jesus, help me to spread thy fragrance everywhere I go.
Flood my soul with thy spirit and love.
Penetrate and possess my whole being so utterly that all my life may only be a radiance of thine.
Shine through me and be so in me that every soul I come in contact with may feel thy presence in my soul.
Let them look up and see no longer me but only Jesus.
Stay with me and then I shall begin to shine as you shine, so to shine as to be a light to others.

—Prayer of Blessed Mother Teresa of Calcutta[48]

---

48 http://www.americancatholic.org/Features/Teresa/Prayer.asp.

Chapter 26
Working with Others and Working Smart

A spirituality of communion means, finally, to know how to "make room" for our brothers and sisters, bearing "each other's burdens" (Galatians 6:2) and resisting the selfish temptations which constantly beset us and provoke competition, careerism, distrust and jealousy. Let us have no illusions: unless we follow this spiritual path, external structures of communion will serve very little purpose. They would become mechanisms without a soul, "masks" of communion rather than its means of expression and growth.

—St. John Paul II, *Novo Millennio Ineunte*, 43

HOWEVER GOD INSPIRES you to engage in the apostolate of works, it will sooner or later involve partnering with others. You may be moved to make rosaries and send them to persecuted Christians; you may be inspired to join your parish's efforts to alleviate poverty in a nearby city; you may feel a call to work full-time as a youth minister or part-time as a Catholic summer camp director; you may be nudged by the Holy Spirit to dedicate all your professional expertise to solving a major humanitarian crisis, like the lack of clean water in some third-world region; you may discover in your heart a burning desire to found a new Catholic research institute dedicated to figuring out how to evangelize the digital continent. Whatever form your apostolate of works takes, you will have to partner with other people in order to fulfill the dream that God planted in your soul. That's just how it is. As Christians, we are never Lone Rangers.

The Gospel Isn't Individualistic

Some modern cultures tend to be exceedingly individualistic. Christians in those contexts often prefer an individualistic apostolate—something they can control and keep within the bounds of their comfort zone. But the work of the Church is always the work of the *Church*. From his encounter with the very first disciples, Jesus called his followers to work in teams. He formed a team of twelve apostles to be his immediate successors in building the Church. And even when he sent out the seventy-two disciples, he sent them out into the villages "two by two" (Luke 10:1).

This was intentional. It reflects the truth of our human nature, as created in God's own image. God, to put it in overly simplistic terms, is a team: Father, Son, and Holy Spirit. And so we, who are called to image God here on earth, live and work and do apostolate not just as individuals, but as members of a community, a team.

The Call to Communion

The theological term most often used to refer to this essential mark of Christian life is *communion*.

> *To make the Church the home and the school of communion: that is the great challenge facing us in the millennium which is now beginning, if we wish to be faithful to God's plan and respond to the world's deepest yearnings…. Before making practical plans, we need to promote a spirituality of communion…. Communion must be cultivated and extended day by day and at every level in the structures of each Church's life. There, relations between Bishops, priests and deacons, between Pastors and the entire People of God, between clergy and Religious, between associations and*

ecclesial movements must all be clearly characterized by communion…. The theology and spirituality of communion encourage a fruitful dialogue between Pastors and faithful: on the one hand uniting them a priori in all that is essential, and on the other leading them to pondered agreement in matters open to discussion.[49]

God has not created us self-sufficient, but interdependent. Each individual and each community has something unique to contribute to the mosaic of the Church as a whole, and no one person or single group can fulfill the mission of evangelization all alone.

Working with others always brings challenges. Sometimes it seems so much easier just to launch out on our own and make things happen. Sometimes it seems that the community structure of the Church, with its parishes and dioceses and the proper authorities that go with those entities, is more of an obstacle than a support. And yet this is how God wants us to live and work. Evangelization isn't just a technological challenge whose solution can be engineered through raw creativity and hard work. Evangelization is a journey, a pilgrimage of faith undertaken by the entire people of God. By facing the challenges of working in teams and staying plugged into the broader ecclesial realities, we help avoid fruitless deviations that on the surface may appear to be shortcuts.

Don't Be Afraid of Renewal!

This doesn't mean that we are meant to put up with archaic or dysfunctional patterns of behavior. If a team is unhealthy, we shouldn't just grin and bear it. Seeking constructive ways to renew and reform whatever needs to be renewed and reformed is an important expression of love. Permanent indifference or avoidance in the face of dysfunction is the opposite of love. It breeds cynicism, contempt, and resentment, in addition to inhibiting—or even

---

49 St. John Paul II, *Novo Millennio Ineunte,* 43, 45.

poisoning—apostolic efforts. "Don't be afraid of the renewal of structures!" Pope Francis exhorted in one of his daily homilies.[50]

Learning from the Children of This World

Whether your apostolate takes place within an official Church structure or not, you can benefit from the best practices applicable to every human group and endeavor. The virtue of prudence involves taking time to build and maintain a healthy team—a healthy communion of persons. It involves taking the time and effort to reflect, plan, evaluate, organize, coordinate with other groups and apostolates, communicate, set goals, and invest time and resources wisely. No human enterprise can flourish without such prudence, and although the apostolate is not *merely* a human enterprise, the human factor is real.

When the Holy Spirit moves us to engage in apostolic activity, he doesn't want us to shelve our intelligence and common sense; instead he wants us to baptize and contribute them to the mission. Jesus actually complained to his followers about the tendency we all have to over-spiritualize our apostolic activity, as if by a sheer act of faith we will be able to bypass the normal requirements for effective action. "For the children of this world are more prudent in dealing with their own generation than are the children of light" (Luke 16:8).

Thinking that God will make everything work out even if we are careless and irresponsible in doing our part is a naïve form of fideism (i.e., an exaggerated reliance on faith to the imprudent exclusion of reason). Human efficiency alone can bear no fruit for Christ's kingdom—"Without me you can do nothing," Jesus reminds us (John 15:5)—but human efficiency is a beautiful offering, a concrete expression of love we can place upon the altar and entrust to the Lord's care—just as we use beautiful vessels

---

50 http://www.news.va/en/news/pope-francis-the-holy-spirit-renews-our-lives.

and vestments for the celebration of Mass, not just paper cups and rags. Love moves us to give our best to the beloved. By calling us to share in his redeeming mission, Jesus generously gives us the chance to love him in that way, too.

Questions for Personal Reflection or Group Discussion

1. What idea in this chapter struck you most and why?

2. When you face the challenges of living your mission together with others, how do you tend to react? Why?

3. What challenges are you facing right now in your efforts to engage in apostolic works? How would Jesus want you to deal with those challenges?

4. In every period of Church history, God sparks spiritual and apostolic renewal by raising up new spiritual families within the larger family of the Church. In the Middle Ages the monastic orders emerged, followed by the mendicant orders (Franciscans, Dominicans, and others). As the modern world emerged, more active associations and congregations sprang up. The great saints who began these works of renewal almost always did so by building *communities* of people whom God had inspired with similar desires and sensitivities—the Benedictines, the Jesuits, the Missionaries of Charity. In our period of Church history, God continues to work this way, raising up new movements and calling people to join them and thereby put their lives more concretely at the service of the Church's mission. What will you do today to contribute to these efforts?

•   I will renew my own commitment to an apostolate I know God is inspiring me to be a part of.

- I will begin looking around to find an apostolate or a Catholic faith-community that resonates with me.

- I will renew my commitment to being an active member of my parish community.

- (Write your own resolution) I will_____

Concluding Prayer

O God, You are our Creator. You are good and Your mercy knows no bounds. To You arises the praise of every creature. O God, You have given us an inner law by which we must live. To do Your will is our task. To follow Your ways is to know peace of heart. To You we offer our homage. Guide us on all the paths we travel upon this earth. Free us from all the evil tendencies which lead our hearts away from Your will. Never allow us to stray from You. O God, judge of all humankind, help us to be included among Your chosen ones on the last day. O God, Author of peace and justice, give us true joy and authentic love, and a lasting solidarity among peoples. Give us Your everlasting gifts. Amen!

—St. John Paul II[51]

---

51 *The Pope Speaks* 37/4, 1992, 213; https://www.ewtn.com/JohnPaul2/writings/prayers/guidance.htm).

PART IV
What to Expect

"Go on your way; behold, I am sending you like lambs among wolves. Carry no money bag, no sack, no sandals; and greet no one along the way. Into whatever house you enter, first say, 'Peace to this household.' If a peaceful person lives there, your peace will rest on him; but if not, it will return to you. Stay in the same house and eat and drink what is offered to you, for the laborer deserves his payment. Do not move about from one house to another. Whatever town you enter and they welcome you, eat what is set before you, cure the sick in it and say to them, 'The kingdom of God is at hand for you.' Whatever town you enter and they do not receive you, go out into the streets and say, 'The dust of your town that clings to our feet, even that we shake off against you.' Yet know this: the kingdom of God is at hand. I tell you, it will be more tolerable for Sodom on that day than for that town."

—Luke 10:3–12

Chapter 27
Facing Your Challenges

In this regard our age of profound change is not without grave difficulties for the Church. We who have, together with the whole College of Bishops, "anxiety for all the churches" and preoccupation for their immediate future, are well aware of this. But at the same time, being supported by faith and hope which does not disappoint us, we are sure that grace will not fail the Christian people, and we hope that they themselves will not fail grace, or reject—as some today are gravely tempted to do—the inheritance of truth and holiness handed down to this decisive moment in the history of the world. And this is the point—we think that we have every reason to have confidence in Christian youth: youth will not fail the Church if within the Church there are enough older people able to understand it, to love it, to guide it and to open up to it a future by passing on to it with complete fidelity the Truth which endures. Then new workers, resolute and fervent, will in their turn enter upon spiritual and apostolic work in the fields which are white and ready for the harvest. Then the sower and the reaper will share the same joy of the kingdom.

—Blessed Paul VI, *Gaudete in Domino*

SOMETIMES WE MAY wonder why God decided to burden us with this work of evangelization. Why doesn't he just do it all himself, miraculously, as he did at the wedding feast in Cana?

It's because God made us with a purpose, an existential need to have an impact in the world, to make a difference. And we long for that. To make a lasting difference helps give meaning to our lives, and we yearn for meaning. This mission, this call, this cooperation with the Lord in evangelizing the world is an incomparable path of meaning.

Leaving a Lasting Mark

Pope Benedict XVI beautifully described this yearning and its proper place of fulfillment just a few days before he was elected pope in a passage we have already encountered:

> *All people desire to leave a lasting mark. But what endures? Money does not. Even buildings do not, nor books. After a certain time, longer or shorter, all these things disappear. The only thing that lasts for ever is the human soul, the human person created by God for eternity. The fruit that endures is therefore all that we have sown in human souls: love, knowledge, a gesture capable of touching hearts, words that open the soul to joy in the Lord. So let us go and pray to the Lord to help us bear fruit that endures. Only in this way will the earth be changed from a valley of tears to a garden of God.*[52]

No greater fulfillment exists than the fulfillment that comes from loving God with all our heart, soul, mind, and strength and loving our neighbors as ourselves, and nothing achieves that more than evangelization through our way of life, our words, and our works.

Why Blessings Sometimes Feel Like Burdens

But even so, heeding this call to "go, therefore, and make disciples of all nations" (Matthew 28:19) can feel more like a burden than a blessing. It feels that way because part of our fallen human nature resists our true calling, and that fallen nature is egged on by some of the standards

---

52 Joseph Cardinal Ratzinger, homily, April 18, 2005; (http://www.vatican.va/gpll/documents/homily-pro-eligendo-pontifice_20050418_en.html).

and behavior patterns present in this fallen world, as well as by the influence of our ancient enemy, the devil, and his minions. Loving as Christ loves brings us fulfillment, but it also encounters resistance.

We need to be prepared for that. It shouldn't surprise us. When internal problems and dysfunctions keep cropping up among our fellow apostles or evangelization team, when external obstacles ceaselessly batter our most sincere apostolic efforts, when opposition arises and difficulties present themselves from the most surprisingly and even seemingly contradictory sources—this is nothing to be disoriented by; it is par for the course, the Lord knows all about it, and he can handle it.

"Go on your way; behold, I am sending you like lambs among wolves…. I have told you this so that you may not fall away. They will expel you from the synagogues; in fact, the hour is coming when everyone who kills you will think he is offering worship to God…. In the world you will have trouble, but take courage, I have conquered the world." (Luke 10:3, John 16:1–2, 33)

St. Paul's Troubles

St. Paul is known throughout the history of Christian literature as the apostle par excellence. His tireless journeying to spread the message of Christ yielded amazing results and indeed planted the seeds of Christian civilization. When you visit the city of Rome today, you see towering statues and gorgeous monuments dedicated to his pioneering work of evangelization. From the perspective offered by twenty centuries of Christian living, we can clearly see the amazing magnitude of his achievement. We should be inspired by that and give glory to God for it, as Christians have done since the first centuries of our era.

And yet, during the period when he was actually engaged in his evangelizing labors, such glorious success often eluded him. His life unfolded amid constant opposition, persecution, difficulties, challenges, misunderstandings, and, yes, even failures. God was working in him and through him, but the process was not some meteoric rise to glory. Rather, it followed the rhythms of Christ's own life: normal Nazareth, dramatic public life, painful passion, glorious resurrection. All these elements were present throughout his missionary life, and they will all be present throughout our missionary lives, too. We must be ready for that.

In the following passage, St. Paul paints a portrait of what it was like for him to faithfully answer the Lord's call in his life. He issues this enumeration as a self-defense (which he was reluctant to give, but it was necessary) against unjust critics who were maligning him and trying to undermine his apostolic toils:

> *Are they ministers of Christ? (I am talking like an insane person.) I am still more, with far greater labors, far more imprisonments, far worse beatings, and numerous brushes with death. Five times at the hands of the Jews I received forty lashes minus one. Three times I was beaten with rods, once I was stoned, three times I was shipwrecked, I passed a night and a day on the deep; on frequent journeys, in dangers from rivers, dangers from robbers, dangers from my own race, dangers from Gentiles, dangers in the city, dangers in the wilderness, dangers at sea, dangers among false brothers; in toil and hardship, through many sleepless nights, through hunger and thirst, through frequent fastings, through cold and exposure. And apart from these things, there is the daily pressure upon me of my anxiety for all the churches. Who is weak, and I am not weak? Who is led to sin, and I am not indignant? (2 Corinthians 11:23–29)*

The Christian mission, the Christian life with its priestly, prophetic, and kingly dimensions, always bears the sign of its Lord and Savior:

the Sign of the Cross. Let's decide ahead of time— right now in fact—that we won't let it confuse us.

Questions for Personal Reflection or Group Discussion

1. What idea in this chapter struck you most and why?

2. If we are created to evangelize, to love God and neighbor, why does it often feel so difficult to do? Explain that apparent contradiction in your own words.

3. When have you experienced the blessings that come from evangelizing? Remember, savor, and thank God for that. When have you experienced the burden of evangelizing? Remember, accept, and thank God for that as well.

4. Our attitude toward the crosses that come into our lives, the troubles and sufferings and difficulties that grate on us and weigh us down, is an important aspect of our spiritual life. The crosses don't come *in spite of* God's love for us; they are somehow mysteriously part of his plan for us, just as the passion and crucifixion of Jesus was part of the Father's plan for redeeming the world. What will you do today to embrace your crosses with faith and love?

- I will make the Sign of the Cross slowly, intentionally, and prayerfully before I pray.

- I will spend a few minutes gazing at my crucifix, and then I will thank Jesus for loving me so much that he was willing to suffer the attacks of evil in order to atone for my sins and those of the whole world.

- I will reach out to someone whose cross is heavier than mine right now and try to help that person carry it.

- (Write your own resolution) I will_____

Concluding Prayer

The Lord is my light and my salvation;
whom should I fear?
The Lord is my life's refuge;
of whom should I be afraid?

When evildoers come at me
to devour my flesh,
these my enemies and foes
themselves stumble and fall.

Though an army encamp against me,
my heart does not fear;
Though war be waged against me,
even then do I trust.

For God will hide me in his shelter
in time of trouble,
he will conceal me in the cover of his tent;
and set me high upon a rock.

—Psalm 27:1–3, 5

Chapter 28
Exorcising the Specter of Discouragement

The gospel is certainly demanding. We know that Christ never permitted his disciples and those who listened to him to entertain any illusions about this. On the contrary, he spared no effort in preparing them for every type of internal or external difficulty, always aware of the fact that they might well decide to abandon him. Therefore, if he says, "Be not afraid!" he certainly does not say it in order to nullify in some way that which he has required. Rather, by these words he confirms the entire truth of the gospel and all the demands it contains. At the same time, however, he revealed that his demands never exceed man's abilities. If man accepts these demands with an attitude of faith, he will also find in the grace that God never fails to give him the necessary strength to meet those demands.

—St. John Paul II[53]

DISCOURAGEMENT IS ONE of an apostle's greatest enemies. It can sneak up on us. We need to understand it in order to be ready to resist it. A good place to do so is in chapter 24 of St. Luke's Gospel, where we read the familiar story of the disciples on the road to Emmaus.

It was Easter Sunday. The gruesome events of Good Friday were over, and while the eleven apostles were still hanging

---

53 John Paul II, *Crossing the Threshold of Hope* (New York: Alfred A. Knopf, 1994), p. 222 (emphasis added).

together, the wider circle of disciples was starting to disperse. Two of these, one named Cleopas, were walking from Jerusalem back their hometown of Emmaus.

Along the way they were discussing everything that had happened—the life and teaching of Jesus, his trial and crucifixion, and even the first vague reports of the empty tomb. But it was not a happy, enthusiastic discussion. On the contrary, St. Luke tells us they were "looking downcast." They were disheartened—the Greek word has connotations of gloomy and morose. They were experiencing what all of us experience sooner or later in our faith journey: the suffocating weight of discouragement.

The Role of Sadness

Simple sadness is different than discouragement. Feeling sad is part of being human, and nothing is wrong with that emotion. But when we let the feeling of sadness seep into our hearts and minds and extinguish our hope, when we let it convince us to relinquish our evangelizing efforts, then it becomes a danger, a temptation, a threat to the health of our souls—that's discouragement.

An old saying among spiritual writers claims that discouragement never comes from the Holy Spirit. The emotion of sadness can be in harmony with the Holy Spirit's work in our souls, because this fallen world has legitimate causes for sadness—death, loss, sin, and the destruction that sin wreaks, for example. To be insensitive to those things would be inhuman and spiritually blind.

In his Sermon on the Mount, Jesus proclaimed that experiencing sadness over these kinds of things, a sadness in harmony with truth, helps us move forward on the path of a meaningful life. "Blessed are those who mourn," he taught, "for they will be comforted" (Matthew 5:4).

Jesus himself sometimes experienced profound sadness: He wept over the city of Jerusalem, which refused to receive his message of salvation; he wept over the death of his friend Lazarus;

his soul became "sorrowful even to death" in the Garden of Gethsemane (Mark 14:34).

Defining Discouragement

But that kind of sadness is different than discouragement. Since sadness comes simply from recognizing the brokenness of a fallen world, it doesn't paralyze us and extinguish our hope. Rather, it expresses our love for all that is good and true, for all that sin and evil destroy. This kind of sadness, then, strengthens our hearts against evil and actually feeds our courage.

Discouragement, on the other hand, is sadness gone crazy. Like a wound that has become infected, discouragement is sadness that starts to fester, and it produces spiritual poison. The English word *discouragement* expresses this well. It literally means "without courage." To become discouraged is to lose the energy necessary to continue fighting. To become discouraged is to play with the temptation to give up and give in, to stop trying.

Someone who is discouraged no longer strives after the worthy goal he or she used to believe in, because that person no longer has any hope that goal is attainable. And that is precisely why discouragement can never come from the Holy Spirit—in Christ, with the help of God's grace, every worthy goal is always attainable. As the angel said to the Blessed Virgin Mary during the Annunciation: "For nothing will be impossible with God" (Luke 1:37). And Jesus himself said the same thing: "For human beings this is impossible, but for God all things are possible" (Matthew 19:26). That's why discouragement always hides some kind of lie.

The Expectation Trap

These two disciples, then, were dragging their feet toward Emmaus, with long faces and downcast hearts. They were in a dangerous situation, spiritually speaking: They were discouraged.

At that point Jesus came up and started walking beside

them, although they didn't recognize him. Jesus asked them what they were talking about, and in their explanation of the recent events, they revealed why they were discouraged. After recounting all the wonderful things Jesus had done and the horrible tragedy of his betrayal, crucifixion, and death, they said, "But we were hoping that he would be the one to redeem Israel" (Luke 24:21).

"We were hoping," the two disciples admit. They had hoped in Jesus, but now their hope had died. They had expected so much from him, even changing their lives to follow him, but now their expectations had been shattered, and they were returning to the way things had been.

We have all had that experience. We have expected God to act in a certain way in our life or give us a certain kind of apostolic success, and then had the wind knocked out of us when those expectations were not met. We have all felt the disappointment, the confusion, the frustration—the *discouragement*—that can come with shattered expectations.

The Real Cause of Discouragement

Up to that point in the conversation, Jesus had simply been listening. But once they finished their story, he chimed in with some words that didn't appear to be very comforting, at least not at first: "O how foolish you are!" (Luke 24:25) He called them fools! Most likely he said it with a smile and not a frown, but even so, we can only imagine the shocked look on the faces of these two disciples when this apparent stranger, instead of commiserating with them, upbraided them.

And then Jesus went on to explain *why* they were being foolish, and in so doing, he revealed the real cause of every discouragement, of every festering sadness that threatens to extinguish our hope, paralyze our souls, and halt the advance of evangelization.

O, how foolish you are! How slow of heart to believe in all that the prophets spoke! Was it not necessary that the

Messiah should suffer these things and enter into his glory?
(Luke 24:25, emphasis added)

There it is, the source of all spiritual discouragement: a faltering faith, an unwillingness to believe in God's way of doing things, a reluctance to accept the revealed truth that all salvation, all growth in holiness, all progress in spiritual maturity, and all apostolic fruitfulness must pass along the way of the cross. When things go wrong, it doesn't mean God has abandoned us—the Crucifixion isn't the end of the story; the Resurrection is.

Adjusting Expectations

When we expect life to be without the cross, our expectations are false, and they will always end up being shattered. The cross was necessary, Jesus emphasized; it was somehow part of God's plan that the new and eternal life shining out on Easter Sunday should rise from the hideous and painful darkness of Good Friday.

This is true for our own spiritual lives, and it is also true for our evangelizing efforts. Jesus summarized it with one of his favorite images, that of a seed: "Amen, amen, I say to you, unless a grain of wheat falls to the ground and dies, it remains just a grain of wheat; but if it dies, it produces much fruit" (John 12:24).

And throughout the history of the Church, that saying has been verified, over and over again. As the early Christian theologian Tertullian put it, "The blood of the martyrs is the seed of the Church."[54] And since our evangelization efforts are all about spreading and growing the Church, we need not be discouraged when those efforts require our blood—on the contrary, we should rejoice: "Now I rejoice in my sufferings for your sake, and in my flesh I am filling up what is lacking in the afflictions of Christ on behalf of his body, which is the church" (Colossians 1:24).

---

54 Tertullian, *Apologeticum*, chapter 50; http://www.tertullian.org/works/apologeticum.htm.

Questions for Personal Reflection or Group Discussion

1. What idea in this chapter struck you most and why?

2. What do you usually do when you experience healthy sadness? How can you better integrate those experiences into your prayer life?

3. When do you tend to get discouraged and why? How do you usually react to discouragement? How can you infuse more faith into those reactions?

4. In order to integrate our emotions into our spiritual life in a healthy way, we first have to learn to identify and own up to what we feel—to "name and claim" our feelings. Taking some time each day to pray what is traditionally called an "examination of conscience" is a good way to do this. In this type of prayer, we quiet our souls and then reflect on how we have been living the events of daily life. We ask God to enlighten us about how he has been present and how we have been responding to the opportunities and challenges his providence has been dishing up. In that atmosphere of reflective prayer, we can often begin to see our own emotional reaction patterns and start to understand them better. What will you do today to increase your self-knowledge?

• I will start—or jump-start—a daily examination of conscience, looking for a guide to help me if necessary.[55]

• I will take some time during the following four Sundays to write in a spiritual journal, trying to describe what is happening in my soul and how I am dealing with that.

---

55 The conference video from the retreat guide, *Sitting in the Side Pew,* gives some pointers about how to do this kind of prayer: http://rcspirituality.org/sitting-in-the-side-pew-conference-video/.

- I will find a good book on my vocation (marriage, priesthood, consecrated life), and I will read it with an eye to better understanding God's point of view regarding my state in life and how I can better live in harmony with that.

- (Write your own resolution) I will_____

Concluding Prayer

The Lord is my shepherd;
there is nothing I lack.
In green pastures he makes me lie down;
to still waters he leads me;

He restores my soul.
He guides me along right paths
for the sake of his name.

Even though I walk through the valley of the shadow of death,
I will fear no evil, for you are with me;
your rod and your staff comfort me.

You set a table before me
in front of my enemies;
You anoint my head with oil;
my cup overflows.

Indeed, goodness and mercy will pursue me
all the days of my life;
I will dwell in the house of the Lord
for endless days.

—Psalm 23

Chapter 29
The Perennial Pitfall

It is important however that what we propose, with the help of God, should be profoundly rooted in contemplation and prayer. Ours is a time of continual movement which often leads to restlessness, with the risk of "doing for the sake of doing." We must resist this temptation by trying "to be" before trying "to do." In this regard we should recall how Jesus reproved Martha: "You are anxious and troubled about many things; one thing is needful" *(Luke 10:41–42).*

—St. John Paul II, *Novo Millennio Ineunte*, 15

ONE OF THE perennial pitfalls for Christian apostles is activism. Activism is idolizing our evangelizing activities, behaving and thinking as if we ourselves were the redeemers of the world and not Jesus.

Getting Things Done

Some personalities have a built-in propensity for this—they just want to get things done and have no patience for delays of any kind. For others the temptation flows more from the depth of their love: They see how much need the world has for God's grace and thus keep overcommitting themselves, taking on way more responsibilities and projects than they can effectively handle.

That is a formula for burnout and can serve as a back door for the devil—he can no longer make any progress by tempting someone with mortal sin and outright rebellion against God, so he sneaks in under the radar, stimulating thoughts that appear to be holy *(You need to do more for the Lord! Don't you love him? Isn't there more you can do?)* only to use them as a disguise for spiritual pride *(I really have to do this, that, and the other thing, even though my health and my family life and my prayer life are collapsing—if I don't do all these projects, I will be letting God down, and there is no one else who can possibly do them)*.

Activism can have truly horrendous consequences. Those who were formerly full of sincere zeal for Christ and his kingdom can become bitter and resentful toward God. They can blame the very people they used to work with in their evangelizing efforts for their own ennui and exhaustion, feeding sentiments of anger as well as violent and destructive criticism. They can even begin to direct their previously apostolic energies toward quixotic causes they believe are necessary to fix all the Church's problems— the problems that, they claim, led to the painful burnout they experienced.

Staying Close to the Vine

One giveaway for creeping activism is usually linked to our prayer life. Prayer always must be our first priority. Without a healthy life of prayer—including vocal prayer, mental prayer, and the sacraments of the Eucharist and confession—our relationship with God will surely languish, and then what do we have to give to others? Unless we keep filling our own souls with God's grace and strength, we quickly run out of the necessary supplies for effective evangelization. As Jesus said: "You are the salt of the earth. But if salt loses its taste, with what can it be seasoned? It is no longer good for anything but to be thrown out and trampled underfoot" (Matthew 5:13).

The apostolic fruit our Christian lives are called to bear is a supernatural fruit. When we cut ourselves off from its source by skimping on our prayer life, we invite barrenness.

"Remain in me, as I remain in you. Just as a branch cannot bear fruit on its own unless it remains on the vine, so neither can you unless you remain in me. I am the vine, you are the branches. Whoever remains in me and I in him will bear much fruit, because without me you can do nothing. Anyone who does not remain in me will be thrown out like a branch and wither; people will gather them and throw them into a fire and they will be burned. If you remain in me and my words remain in you, ask for whatever you want and it will be done for you. By this is my Father glorified, that you bear much fruit and become my disciples." (John 15:4–8)

The evangelizing power of our way of living, the effectiveness of our words of witness, and the success of our apostolic works (the "fruit" Jesus speaks of) all depend primarily on God's grace, because they are all directed toward helping people hear his voice in their lives and respond generously to it. Only a healthy life of prayer can keep that grace flowing through our spiritual veins. Pope Benedict XVI made this point explicitly:

Prayer, as a means of drawing ever new strength from Christ, is concretely and urgently needed. People who pray are not wasting their time, even though the situation appears desperate and seems to call for action alone.... It is time to reaffirm the importance of prayer in the face of the activism and the growing secularism of many Christians engaged in charitable work.[56]

Watching the Stress Meter

Another indicator that activism may be on the rise has to do with

---

56 Pope Benedict XVI, *Deus Caritas Est,* 36, 37.

the experience of anxiety or stress. When we begin depending excessively on our own efforts in order to build up Christ's kingdom, the pressure becomes unbearable. Our efforts will never be sufficient to save the world. Our efforts will never be sufficient to earn God's unconditional love (we already *have* that as a pure gift from God). If we put those kinds of burdens on ourselves, they constrict our soul and drain it of joy. God is the author of salvation and the real protagonist in every apostolic endeavor. His invitation to join him in the work of redemption flows from the love he already has for us. If we keep that in mind, it's much harder to lose our sense of joy and enthusiasm.

> *Though it is true that this mission demands great generosity on our part, it would be wrong to see it as a heroic individual undertaking, for it is first and foremost the Lord's work, surpassing anything which we can see and understand. Jesus is "the first and greatest evangelizer." In every activity of evangelization, the primacy always belongs to God, who has called us to cooperate with him and who leads us on by the power of his Spirit. The real newness is the newness which God himself mysteriously brings about and inspires, provokes, guides and accompanies in a thousand ways. The life of the Church should always reveal clearly that God takes the initiative, that "he has loved us first" (1 John 4:19) and that he alone "gives the growth" (1 Corinthians 3:7). This conviction enables us to maintain a spirit of joy in the midst of a task so demanding and challenging that it engages our entire life. God asks everything of us, yet at the same time he offers everything to us.[57]*

In all our evangelizing efforts, a continual purification of our intention is a strong help against falling into the perennial pitfall of activism. What are we truly seeking: to glorify God and help our

---

57 Pope Francis, *Evangelii Gaudium,* 12.

neighbors and thereby fulfill the true meaning of our lives, or to win popularity contests and achievement competitions? Continually and purposely purifying our intention helps us maintain a healthy balance in our lives, giving proper attention to our circles of influence and keeping us docile to God's direction. He is the one in charge of keeping the big picture in mind. Each of us simply needs to listen closely to what he is asking of us and make a decent effort to do that. We are not responsible for saving the world; we are only responsible for doing our part.

Questions for Personal Reflection or Group Discussion

1. What idea in this chapter struck you most and why?

2. In your own life, what are the signs that usually indicate you are falling into your own perennial pitfall?

3. What can you do to keep God first and to increase your trust in him so that you don't put undue pressure on yourself to save the world?

4. As we saw in chapter 7, the Christian way of life is meant to be a balanced and fruitful way of life. It can't turn earth into heaven—we will always have to face challenges and problems—but growth in spiritual maturity does make us stronger and more stable, more joyful and peaceful, even in the midst of trials and temptations. What will you do today to regain some balance in your life so God's grace can flow more freely in you and through you?

•   I will take a look at what I do for entertainment and cut out any excesses—relaxation is a real human need, but it is not the purpose of my life here on earth.

•   I will reflect on the five most important relationships in my life and see which one is the most neglected. I will make a concrete effort to invest in that relationship this week.

· I will look at my commitments and those of my family. I will divide them into categories—essential, useful, and superfluous. I will then drop the superfluous commitments and resolve to take sufficient time to reflect before making new commitments.

· (Write your own resolution) I will_____.

Concluding Prayer

Holy Mary, Mother of God,
you have given the world its true light,
Jesus, your Son—the Son of God.
You abandoned yourself completely
to God's call
and thus became a wellspring
of the goodness which flows forth from him.
Show us Jesus. Lead us to him.
Teach us to know and love him,
so that we too can become
capable of true love
and be fountains of living water
in the midst of a thirsting world.

—Pope Benedict XVI[58]

---

58 Pope Benedict XVI, *Deus Caritas Est*, 42.

Chapter 30
Avoiding the Rush

This passion will not fail to stir in the Church a new sense of mission, which cannot be left to a group of "specialists" but must involve the responsibility of all the members of the People of God. Those who have come into genuine contact with Christ cannot keep him for themselves, they must proclaim him. A new apostolic outreach is needed, which will be lived as the everyday commitment of Christian communities and groups.... Christ must be presented to all people with confidence. We shall address adults, families, young people, children, without ever hiding the most radical demands of the gospel message, but taking into account each person's needs in regard to their sensitivity and language, after the example of Paul who declared: "I have become all things to all men, that I might by all means save some." (I Corinthians 9:22)

—St. John Paul II, *Novo Millennio Ineunte*, 40

OUR LORD'S FAVORITE images for his kingdom always had to do with plants. The sower who went out to sow, the mustard seed, the grain of wheat, the farmer's field…his kingdom is like that. It grows organically, taking time to put down roots and put up shoots, going through different seasons as its fruit matures. And just as farmers cannot rush their crops but have to respect the natural rhythms of growth, so too Christian apostles need patience and perseverance as they respect the seasons of evangelical growth.

Sharing in the Labor

Sometimes, in fact, we may never see the harvest of the seeds we planted—at least, not this side of heaven. Sometimes we are called to plant, other times to water, and still other times to bring in the harvest. Jesus made this point in a conversation with his disciples:

> *For here the saying is verified that "One sows and another reaps." I sent you to reap what you have not worked for; others have done the work, and you are sharing the fruits of their work. (John 47–48)*

St. Paul picks up on this same image in order to remind the Christians in Corinth that the spiritual fruitfulness they have experienced through believing in the gospel is not the result of merely human activity, and so the men who preached the gospel (in this case Apollos and Paul himself) deserve only relative credit:

> *What is Apollos, after all, and what is Paul? Ministers through whom you became believers, just as the Lord assigned each one. I planted, Apollos watered, but God caused the growth. Therefore, neither the one who plants nor the one who waters is anything, but only God, who causes the growth. The one who plants and the one who waters are equal, and each will receive wages in proportion to his labor. For we are God's co-workers; you are God's field. (1 Corinthians 3:5–9)*

Patience and perseverance do not contradict hard work and a healthy sense of urgency. We are not called to be idle—the Lord sends us into his vineyard every day, and he is really hoping we will strive to do our part: "We have to do the works of the one who sent me while it is day. Night is coming when no one can work"

(John 9:4). But since we are just God's "co-workers," and since it is the Lord who causes the growth, we must adjust our expectations in accordance with his pace and his priorities. That isn't always easy, since we like to see results quickly and dramatically, but for the Lord "one day is like a thousand years and a thousand years are like one day" (2 Peter 3:8).

Seasons of Salvation

Perhaps patience and perseverance are harder for us than they were for Christians in past ages. The pace of life in the digital world is so accelerated and the rate of technological progress so dizzying that we expect quick results, quick fixes, quick progress, and quick resolution. We are products and citizens of an on-demand culture, but spiritual and apostolic growth are not on-demand items—they are seasonal.

Throughout the history of salvation, every major event had its seasons. Moses didn't even begin his mission to free Israel from Egyptian slavery until he was an old man. David had to wait nineteen years—enduring persecution for most of them—between his anointing as the new king of Israel and his actual crowning. Even Jesus, as we have seen, spent thirty years in obscurity before launching out on his public mission, and then he prefaced his first sermon with a forty-day retreat in the desert wilderness. The nascent Church had to wait for seven weeks after the Resurrection before receiving the Holy Spirit at Pentecost. The Church is "God's field," and the fruits of her evangelizing effort take time to mature.

You Cannot Rush the Effects of Grace

Our apostolic activities deserve our best efforts and our smartest strategies, but unlike mere worldly work, their fruits are not completely in our control. To evangelize is to work with God and for God and allow him to arrange the calendar. The effects of grace go beyond our merely human efforts, and we need to learn to be okay with that. Pope Benedict XVI alluded to this principle when visiting the United States, a society where materialism and technocracy have grown to gargantuan proportions, and where the humility necessary for patience and perseverance often can seem in short supply.

> *For an affluent society, a further obstacle to an encounter with the living God lies in the subtle influence of materialism…. It is easy to be entranced by the almost unlimited possibilities that science and technology place before us; it is easy to make the mistake of thinking we can obtain by our own efforts the fulfillment of our deepest needs. This is an illusion. Without God, who alone bestows upon us what we by ourselves cannot attain, our lives are ultimately empty…. The goal of all our pastoral and catechetical work, the object of our preaching, and the focus of our sacramental ministry should be to help people establish and nurture that living relationship with "Christ Jesus, our hope." (1 Timothy 1:1)*

Evangelization seeks to "establish and nurture" a living relationship between God and every person, and relationships always take time to develop. This apostolate poses many practical challenges, which we should meet with all the creativity and energy we would apply to any practical challenge. But the central challenge is actually deeper; it involves healing broken hearts and sickened souls, and those things cannot be rushed.

Yearning of Love versus Worldly Rush

Jesus felt the urgent yearning of love; it burned in his heart like a fire: "I have come to set the earth on fire, and how I wish it were already blazing!" (Luke 12:49) But when he commissioned his followers to make disciples of all nations, he let them know how long it would take to finish: "And behold, I am with you always, until the end of the age" (Matthew 28:20). The evangelizing mission of the Church will continue until the end of history. It is the cultivation of a kingdom that grows like a farmer's field. Let's work hard, planting and watering and weeding however the Lord asks us to, but let's do so calmly and wisely, trusting first and foremost in him and his love, not in our human smarts and strengths. Let's avoid the worldly rush and make room for the flow of grace.

Be patient, therefore, brothers, until the coming of the Lord. See how the farmer waits for the precious fruit of the earth, being patient with it until it receives the early and the late rains. You too must be patient. (James 5:7–8)

Questions for Personal Reflection or Group Discussion

1. What idea in this chapter struck you most and why?

2. When do you tend to get impatient and why? How do you usually respond to that? How would you like to respond?

3. When have you been surprised by how God's grace works? Remember, savor, and speak to God about that experience. What do you think he wants you to learn from it?

4. We are responsible for our input into the work of evangelization God invites us to undertake. But God is responsible for the output. What will you do today to cultivate a humble sense of detachment from visible results and a joyful trust in the fruitfulness of every effort offered to God with love?

- When things don't go my way, I will say a prayer of trust in God.

- When things go my way and I experience a success, no matter how small, I will enjoy the feeling and thank God for it.

- After I do my part, I will say a small prayer commending my efforts to God's care and releasing any self-centered or fear-based expectations I may have regarding the results.

- (Write your own resolution) I will_____

Concluding Prayer

Lord, my heart is not haughty,
I do not set my sights too high.
I have taken no part in great affairs,
in wonders beyond my scope.
No, I hold myself in quiet and silence,
like a little child in its mother's arms,
like a little child, so I keep myself.
Let Israel hope in the Lord
henceforth and for ever.

—Psalm 131[59]

---

59 Adapted from the New Jerusalem Bible translation.

Conclusion

THERE IS WORK to do for Christ and his kingdom, and the Lord has invited each one of us to join in it. No other work can ever be as meaningful. As members of the Church, we have been especially equipped for this work of evangelization through the gifts of grace and of the Holy Spirit—we have been commissioned as Christ's messengers and witnesses, as his apostles.

Our apostolic action is priestly, and thus our way of living daily life can become a field of redemption and a channel of grace when we offer it to God and infuse it with Christian intentionality and virtue. This includes the witness of our moral integrity, our kindness, our active love for the Church, and the pursuit of excellence in all that we do.

Our apostolic action is also prophetic: We are called to speak forth the message of Jesus, to spread and explain the teachings of his Church so other people can hear and believe in Christ's truth and become his followers. The example of our daily life is not enough to help people make their way to friendship with Jesus; we must also talk about the Lord.

And our apostolic action is kingly, in the sense that we are called to bring Christian values and order—the law of Christ—into play in every sector of human society. We are ambassadors of the eternal King, and so we share, in a certain sense, in his own authority. We use that authority to shape the events and institutions of this world—starting with those closest to home, but reaching out as far as the Lord inspires us to—in accordance with God's wisdom.

If every Catholic were keenly aware of and deeply committed to these fundamental truths about our Christian identity, the world would be a very different place. Let's go and make that happen!

Then Jesus approached and said to them, "All power in heaven and on earth has been given to me. Go, therefore, and make disciples of all nations, baptizing them in the name of the Father, and of the Son, and of the holy Spirit, teaching them to observe all that I have commanded you. And behold, I am with you always, until the end of the age." (Matthew 28:18–20)

Acknowledgments

This book would not have been possible without the collaboration of a vast team of fellow pilgrims, especially the following, whom I want to thank sincerely: Fr. John Connor, Debra Graspointner, Dianne Hart, Lucy Honner, Fr. Steven Liscinsky, Jennifer Meyer, DJ Venne and the whole team at Ministry23, Claudia Volkman, the Cupertino, California, community of Legionaries of Christ, and the fledging "Writers' Team" who took joyful advantage of their hospitality.

The Complete Christian Series

Go! 30 Meditations on How Best to Love Your Neighbor as Yourself is the third book in Father John Bartunek's **Complete Christian Series**. This series guides you to encounter Christ in *The Better Part*, become His loving disciple in *Seeking First the Kingdom*, and live out your missionary vocation in *Go!*

To order, call 1-800-932-3051 or visit CatholicWord.com

The Better Part +
A Guide to Christian Meditation

Meet Christ in this Gospel-centered resource and daily meditation companion. All four Gospels are contained within the text and brought to new light through Fr. Bartunek's illuminating commentary.

Seeking First the Kingdom:
30 Meditations on How to Love God with All Your Heart, Soul, Mind, and Strength

Learn how to bring every dimension of your being into your relationship with God, how to handle the emotional roller coaster of everyday life, and how to overcome spiritual obstacles and roadblocks.